LIBERTY & THE INK WELL

A Guided Journey Through America's Founding Principles

By: Ron Coleman

"To the citizens of this great nation —
from the fields to the factories,
from the highways to the hearths.
May we never forget that liberty lives
in the people."

———

Grey Wolf Press
An Independent American Publisher
GreyWolfPress.net

Printed in the United States of America

First Edition, 2025

ISBNs
Paperback: **979-8-9937521-8-1**
Hardcover: **979-8-9937521-9-8**

Cover Design: by the author
Interior Layout: by the author

About This Book

Liberty & the Ink Well — A Guided Journey Through America's Founding Principles

They didn't just write a nation — they forged it in debate, ink, and courage.

This book brings readers face to face with the original documents that built the United States — the Declaration, the Articles, the Constitution, and the Bill of Rights. Each chapter combines history, trivia, and guided reflection to reveal not only what they wrote, but why it mattered.

Part lesson, part journal, part challenge, *Liberty & the Ink Well* turns America's founding papers into a living conversation about duty, freedom, and faith in self-government.

Because liberty isn't preserved by memory alone —
it endures when we understand it.

Table of Contents

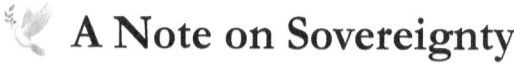 A Note on Sovereignty

Sovereignty is one of the most misunderstood ideas in American life — yet it is the key that unlocks every page of this book.

For most of human history, sovereignty belonged to kings, emperors, parliaments, and distant rulers. It meant the ultimate authority to govern, to command, and to decide the fate of a nation.

The American Founders reversed that order.

In the United States, **sovereignty rests not with the government or the country, but with the people** — a radical idea in 1776, and still a revolutionary idea today.
It means:

- Government derives its power *from the consent of the governed.*

- Citizens are not subjects, but the source of all legitimate authority.

- Rights do not flow downward from rulers — they rise upward from the people.

Every document in this book — the Declaration, the Articles, the Constitution, and the Bill of Rights — is rooted in that single truth:
A free nation is one in which the people themselves hold the highest power.

As you read, remember this:
When the Constitution speaks of "the people," it is not speaking about institutions or officials.
It is speaking about you.

Sovereignty is not a theory.
It is a responsibility — the first principle of liberty, and the one that keeps the Republic alive.

✏ Author's Note

America was not shaped by perfect men, but by determined ones.
Men who argued, prayed, disagreed, and kept moving forward because
the future of liberty depended on it. As I studied their words and
walked the miles of my own journey, I learned something simple but
profound: freedom is not a gift we inherit — it is a responsibility we
accept.

This book is not meant to lecture, but to invite.
To invite you to *think*, to question, to write, and to reflect on the
principles that built our Republic. The Founders didn't ask us to admire
them; they asked us to remember what they fought for — and to keep it
alive.

Much of this book was something I thought of while on the road — in
truck stops, quiet campsites, parking lots under starlit skies, and long
stretches of American highway. The conversations I had with farmers,
veterans, truckers, and families shaped these pages as much as any
document from 1776. Their voices reminded me that liberty lives in
ordinary people doing extraordinary things — sometimes simply by
speaking up, praying boldly, or standing firm when it would be easier to
sit down.

If these pages strengthen your love for our Constitution, deepen your
gratitude for the freedoms we share, or spark a single meaningful
conversation, then the effort was worth it.

Thank you for taking this journey through America's founding
principles with me.
The road taught me many lessons — but the greatest was this:

Freedom endures when the people choose to carry it.
And today, that includes you.

— *Ron Coleman*
Nevada

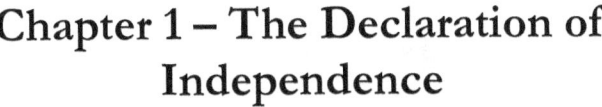

Chapter 1 – The Declaration of Independence

"That to secure these rights, Governments are instituted among Men..."

— *The Declaration of Independence, 1776*

 **Freedom Fact**

Before the Constitution, the Declaration of Independence was our first great act of unity — not a law, but a *statement of principle* that told the world *who we are* and *why we exist* as a free people.

A Brief Story

In the summer of 1776, tension hung in the air like a storm about to break. Thirteen colonies had grown tired of taxes, distant rulers, and laws passed without their consent.
Fifty-six brave men gathered in Philadelphia and signed their names to a document that could cost them everything — but secure liberty for everyone who would come after.

Thomas Jefferson, just 33 years old, took up his quill and wrote the words that still echo through time:

"We hold these truths to be self-evident, that all men are created equal..."

That sentence became the heartbeat of America.

🕐 Trivia Time

1 **Who was the principal author of the Declaration of Independence?**
Answer: Thomas Jefferson

2 **On what date did the Continental Congress adopt the Declaration?**
Answer: July 4, 1776

3 **Which famous signature is the largest on the Declaration?**
Answer: John Hancock

4 **How many colonies approved the Declaration?**
Answer: Twelve voted yes; New York abstained but later approved.

5 **What did signing the Declaration amount to, legally, under British law?**
Answer: Treason — punishable by death.

6 **Where was the Declaration signed?**
Answer: Independence Hall in Philadelphia, Pennsylvania.

7 **Who was president of the Continental Congress when it was signed?**
Answer: John Hancock

8 **Which future U.S. president and his friend both died on July 4, 1826, the Declaration's 50th anniversary?**
Answer: John Adams and Thomas Jefferson

9 **What powerful closing line appears before the signatures?**
Answer: "We mutually pledge to each other our Lives, our Fortunes and our sacred Honor."

10 **What truth does the Declaration of Independence begin with?**
Answer: "That all men are created equal, endowed by their Creator with certain unalienable Rights…"

A Moment to Reflect

It's said that one of Jefferson's enslaved attendants may have seen or overheard what he was writing and questioned how a man could speak so passionately about liberty while others remained in chains.
Whether that conversation truly happened or not, it captures the great contradiction of America's birth — that freedom was declared in a world that still denied it to many.
Jefferson's words and actions didn't always align, but his pen lit a spark that would one day challenge even the injustice he left unresolved.

Challenge Corner

Imagine standing in Independence Hall in 1776. Would you have signed your name, knowing it might cost you your life?
Talk about it with friends or family. Courage doesn't just belong to the past — it belongs to every generation that chooses to stand for freedom.

Did You Know?

- Jefferson's first draft of the Declaration **condemned slavery**, but Congress removed that section to maintain unity among the colonies.

- Only about **200 copies** of the first printing (the *"Dunlap Broadsides"*) were made — and just **26 are known to survive today.**

- The **Liberty Bell** likely rang on **July 8, 1776**, to announce the first public reading of the Declaration.

Jefferson's Original Condemnation (June 1776 Draft)

Jefferson's draft accused King George III of:

"...waging cruel war against human nature itself, violating its most sacred rights of life and liberty in the persons of a distant people who never offended him, captivating and carrying them into slavery..."

He went further, charging the King with **blocking colonial efforts to end the slave trade**, calling it a *"disgraceful commerce."*

The clause was **struck out** after objections from:

- **South Carolina**

- **Georgia**

- and **some delegates from northern colonies involved in the slave trade**, especially merchants from **Massachusetts and Rhode Island.**

Freedom Reflection

The Declaration wasn't just a break from a king — it was a commitment to a set of ideals.
Equality, liberty, and the belief that rights come from our Creator — not from government.
Every time you read it aloud or hand someone a pocket Constitution, you're carrying that torch forward.

Consent of the Governed

The Founders made it clear that governments exist **only by the consent of the governed** — meaning that power flows upward from *the people*, not downward from rulers.
That was a revolutionary idea in 1776. No kings, no nobles, no divine right of birth.
If a government forgets that its power is borrowed, it loses its legitimacy.
Our leaders are not masters — they are servants, entrusted with temporary authority by free citizens.

When Jefferson wrote that line, he wasn't just speaking about Britain. He was defining what it means to be an American: that freedom depends on our willingness to *watch, question, and hold accountable* those who serve us.

The Right to Alter or Abolish

The Declaration goes even further:

"…That whenever any Form of Government becomes destructive of these ends, it is the Right of the People to alter or to abolish it, and to institute new Government…"

Those words weren't written as a threat — they were written as a reminder.
When a government stops defending liberty and starts destroying it, the people have not only the right, but the **duty**, to change it.
That doesn't always mean revolution or violence — it can mean speaking up, voting, reforming laws, or restoring truth where it's been lost.
The Founders risked everything to prove that the governed are never powerless when united in purpose.

That principle still stands: governments serve at our consent, and we must never forget that consent can be withdrawn when liberty is at stake.

Tidbits about The Declaration Of Independence

1. It's Structured Like a Legal Indictment

The Declaration isn't just a speech — it's a **legal case** against King George III.
It follows the same form as an 18th-century court filing:

- **Preamble:** States the principles of government (*"all men are created equal…"*).

- **List of Grievances:** 27 specific charges against the King.

- **Conclusion:** The formal *"dissolving"* of ties with Britain.

Freedom Fact: Jefferson and Adams both studied law, and the Declaration's structure mirrors the way a lawyer would present evidence to a jury — with "the world" as the jury.

2. The "Laws of Nature and of Nature's God"

That phrase appears right at the start and is incredibly significant.
It means that **our rights come from natural law** — universal moral law — not from government.
This grounded liberty in something *higher than politics*, giving the Founders moral authority to rebel.

Reflection: This is where the Declaration and the later Constitution connect to faith — liberty isn't granted by man; it's *acknowledged* by man.

⚖ 3. The 27 Grievances Are Not Random

They're grouped in three clear categories:

1. **Injustice in governance** (e.g., dissolving legislatures, ignoring laws)

2. **Abuse of military power** (keeping standing armies, quartering troops)

3. **Economic oppression** (taxation without representation, cutting off trade)

☞ **Freedom Fact:** Each grievance begins with "He has…" — intentionally repetitive, like drumbeats of injustice, to drive home the pattern of tyranny.

💥 4. The King, Not Parliament, Was Blamed on Purpose

Jefferson directed the accusations **at King George III**, not the British Parliament.
Why? Because they still wanted to show respect for the British people — this was a break with *the Crown*, not with all of Britain.

☞ *Trivia Question:*
Q: Why did the Declaration address King George III rather than Parliament?
A: To make the break appear as one nation freeing itself from one ruler, not waging war on another people.

5. The Word "Congress" Appears Nowhere in the Text

Even though it was adopted by the Continental Congress, the word "Congress" doesn't appear in the Declaration itself.
Instead, it's signed simply:

"In Congress, July 4, 1776…"

 Freedom Fact: The Declaration speaks with the voice of *"the Representatives of the United States of America, in General Congress assembled."*
It's one of the first official uses of the phrase "United States of America."

6. The Closing Pledge Is More Than Symbolic

"We mutually pledge to each other our Lives, our Fortunes, and our sacred Honor."

That's not poetic fluff — that was a **literal statement of risk.**
Many signers were wealthy men who knew they'd lose everything if the Revolution failed.
Five were captured and tortured; others saw their homes burned.

 Trivia Challenge:
Q: Which signer lost his home and fortune because of his signature?
A: Thomas Nelson Jr. of Virginia — he personally ordered cannons to fire on his own house when it was used by the British.

7. Jefferson's "Capitalization Style" Was Intentional

In the 18th century, writers capitalized words for emphasis — not grammar.
Jefferson capitalized words like *Truths, Rights, Liberty, Happiness* — each one a moral cornerstone.

 Freedom Fact:
Every capitalized word in the Declaration marks a value they saw as *higher law.*

8. It Mentions God Four Times — in Four Different Ways

1. "Nature's God" — as the author of moral law.

2. "Creator" — as the giver of rights.

3. "Supreme Judge of the world" — as the final moral authority.

4. "Divine Providence" — as the protector of their cause.

Reflection:
This wasn't just rebellion; it was a declaration of faith in a moral universe — one where liberty is sacred.

9. The Word "Independence" Appears Only Once

It's easy to forget — the Declaration only uses the word "independent" in the final paragraph, when they officially *declare themselves free and independent states.*

Trivia Question:
Q: How many times does the word "independence" appear in the Declaration?
A: Just once.

10. The Signing Took Months

Most people imagine all the Founders signing on July 4, 1776 — but that's a myth.
Only **John Hancock** and **Charles Thomson** (as secretary) signed that day.
Most others signed on **August 2, 1776**, and a few even later.

Freedom Fact:
The printer John Dunlap worked overnight on July 4–5 to produce the first printed copies — the "Dunlap Broadsides."

The Ink Well

Before the Founders ever wrote a word, they first asked themselves a simple question: *What does freedom mean to me?* Take a moment to answer that same question in your own words. Write a few lines about what freedom looks like in your life, your home, or your community — and why it's worth protecting.

🦅 Patriot's Reflection

Every signature on the Declaration was an act of courage — but also of faith. Faith that a nation could rise not from the command of kings, but from the conviction of ordinary citizens who knew their rights came from God, not government. Those fifty-six men risked their homes, their livelihoods, and their lives so that future generations — *your generation* — would inherit a country where liberty is not a privilege, but a birthright.

They understood something timeless: freedom survives only when the people themselves insist on it. A Republic cannot rest on parchment alone. It lives in the hearts, choices, and courage of its citizens. Each time you read, speak, or defend the principles of the Declaration, you join the same long line of patriots who refused to bow to tyranny.

The Declaration announced our independence, but winning that independence was only the beginning. The Articles of Confederation would test whether thirteen newly free states could stand together — and whether the promise of liberty written in 1776 could endure the storms that followed.

America's story began with bold ink, a brave idea, and a belief in Providence. The next chapter asked an even greater question: could freedom *govern* as well as it could inspire?

Chapter 2 – The Articles of Confederation

The First Experiment in Freedom

"A firm league of friendship…"
— The Articles of Confederation, 1781

 ## Freedom Fact

After declaring independence, America still had no rulebook for how thirteen free states could govern together.
The **Articles of Confederation** became our first national framework — not a strong federal government, but a cautious agreement among sovereign states that feared another king.

A Brief Story

When the guns of the Revolution thundered, the Continental Congress needed unity to wage war and manage supplies.
In 1777, after months of debate, delegates drafted the **Articles of Confederation** — a document meant to bind the thirteen states "in a firm league of friendship."

Each state kept its independence. There was no president, no national court system, and Congress had no power to tax or enforce laws. Every decision required the consent of nearly everyone — a slow, uncertain way to run a war.
Yet somehow, it held. Through courage, improvisation, and faith in Providence, the United States survived its birth under the Articles.

It worked — barely — through the war. The young nation limped along, paying soldiers with promises instead of coin. Congress printed paper money that quickly lost its value. George Washington, then commander-in-chief of the Continental Army, carried the burden of holding the army together through impossible odds.

Before the Revolution, Washington had served as a **colonel in the Virginia militia**, earning respect for his bravery during the French and Indian War. When Congress called upon him in 1775 to lead the Continental Army, he accepted—not for power, but out of duty. By the winter of 1777, that duty was tested beyond imagination.

At **Valley Forge**, Washington's soldiers wrapped **rags around their feet** in place of boots. Many had no coats, and the snow was marked with blood from their frostbitten toes. Disease swept through the camp, and supplies were so scarce that Washington himself wrote to Congress, warning that his army was "on the verge of dissolution."

Still, he refused to give up. He rode among his men daily, encouraging them, praying with them, reminding them why they fought. He told his officers that the cause of liberty was worth every hardship. "Perseverance and spirit," he said, "have done wonders in all ages."

When victory finally came at Yorktown in 1781, it was as much a triumph of endurance as of strategy. But even as the nation celebrated, Washington saw the cracks in its foundation. He knew that freedom without a functioning government was a fragile dream. His reports to Congress urged reform — a stronger union, a system that could feed and pay its soldiers, a nation worthy of the sacrifice made to win it.

By 1783, independence was won, but unity was fraying. Rival states quarreled over trade, currency, and borders. Some refused to contribute money or troops.
Freedom, it turned out, was easier to declare than to manage. The American experiment was alive — but fragile. The question now was whether liberty could hold a divided people together.

🕐 Trivia Time

1 When were the Articles of Confederation adopted?
Answer: 1777 (adopted) — ratified by all thirteen states in 1781.

2 What phrase described the relationship among the states?
Answer: "A firm league of friendship."

3 How many votes did each state have in Congress?
Answer: One vote per state, regardless of size or population.

4 Could Congress collect taxes under the Articles?
Answer: No — it could only request money from the states.

5 Who signed the Articles on behalf of Maryland, the last state to ratify?
Answer: John Hanson — who later became the first "President of Congress" under the Articles.

6 What major success came from the Articles despite their weaknesses?
Answer: The Northwest Ordinance of 1787, which banned slavery in new territories and set rules for statehood.

7 How many branches of government did the Articles create?
Answer: Only one — a unicameral Congress with no executive or judicial branches.

8 What was required to amend the Articles?
Answer: A unanimous vote of all thirteen states.

9 What event finally convinced many leaders that the Articles were failing?
Answer: Shays' Rebellion (1786–1787) — an uprising of Massachusetts farmers protesting tax debt and economic hardship.

10 What meeting was called to fix the Articles but ended up creating the Constitution instead?
Answer: The Constitutional Convention of 1787 in Philadelphia.

A Moment to Reflect

The Founders feared power concentrated in any one place. After all, they had just fought a king.
But in trying to keep government weak, they made it nearly powerless.
No taxes meant no army. No executive meant no one to carry out decisions.
The nation had liberty — but little stability.

Freedom without structure is like a ship without a rudder: it may drift with the wind of good intentions but cannot steer through storms.

Challenge Corner

Imagine you are a delegate in 1786.
Your state is deep in debt, soldiers are unpaid, and trade wars erupt between neighbors.
Would you vote to give Congress more power — risking another "strong government" — or keep the Articles as they are?
Discuss it. What does *true* independence require: freedom from power or freedom through order?

Did You Know?

- **Maryland** was the last to ratify, holding out until western land claims were surrendered.

- Congress could declare war and sign treaties — but couldn't enforce them.

- The Articles produced the **Northwest Ordinance (1787)**, banning slavery in new territories and laying the groundwork for westward expansion.

Freedom Reflection

The Articles of Confederation were a bold first attempt to live self-governed.
They taught America a hard but valuable lesson — that liberty must be joined with responsibility.
Without unity, independence could not last.

Tidbits about The Articles of Confederation

1. "A Firm League of Friendship"

That phrase described the relationship among the thirteen states. Each one kept its sovereignty and independence.

Freedom Fact: The Articles were written in the middle of the Revolution—unity was urgent, but fear of centralized power ran deep.

2. One Branch of Government

The Articles created only a single body: Congress. There was no executive or judicial branch.

Reflection: This design came straight from distrust of kings—better to have too little power than too much.

3. Equal Votes for Unequal States

Every state, large or small, had exactly one vote in Congress. Population didn't matter.

Freedom Fact: Rhode Island's vote weighed as much as Virginia's—proof of early equality among states.

4. No Power to Tax

Congress could only *ask* states for money. Many ignored the requests.

Reflection: Without taxes, the army went unpaid and the nation nearly collapsed under its own debts.

5. Moving Capitals

Because there was no permanent seat of government, Congress met in at least eight cities—Philadelphia, Baltimore, Princeton, and others.

Trivia Question: Q: Which city served as the capital the longest under the Articles?
A: Philadelphia.

6. The Western Lands Dispute

Some states claimed vast western territories; others had none. Maryland refused to ratify until those lands were ceded to the nation.

Freedom Fact: This compromise led to the Northwest Territory—America's first public land system.

7. The Northwest Ordinance of 1787

Despite its flaws, the Articles produced one of America's greatest laws. It banned slavery in new territories and guaranteed public education.

Reflection: Even weak governments can do strong things when guided by principle.

8. The Army in Rags

By war's end, many Continental soldiers were barefoot, wrapping rags around their feet against the snow.

Freedom Fact: Washington's letters begged Congress for supplies; his men's endurance became a legend of sacrifice.

9. Shays' Rebellion — A Wake-Up Call

In 1786, farmers in western Massachusetts, led by Daniel Shays, rose up against heavy taxes and debt. Many were veterans who had fought for liberty only to face foreclosure on their farms.

Freedom Fact: The rebellion shocked the nation. It revealed that the Articles had created a government too weak to maintain order or support its own veterans.

Reflection: Shays' Rebellion became the final alarm bell that pushed the Continental Congress to call for a convention to "revise" the Articles — a meeting that would lead to something far greater: the Constitution.

10. Washington's Reluctant Return

By 1787, George Washington had retired to Mount Vernon, weary of politics and war. But the call for unity would not leave him in peace. The Continental Congress sent delegates to urge him to attend the Constitutional Convention in Philadelphia.

Freedom Fact: When Washington entered the hall, the delegates rose to their feet. As the doors closed behind him, someone called for a vote — and before he could object, he was chosen as **President of the Convention.**

Reflection: Washington accepted without protest, saying little but believing much. His sense of *duty above comfort* guided the assembly from discord toward the structure that would hold the young nation together.

The Ink Well

The Articles of Confederation were a bold first attempt to live self-governed.

They taught America a hard but valuable lesson — that liberty must be joined with responsibility.

Without unity, independence would not last.

Freedom Fact: What Does "Unicameral" Mean?

Under the Articles of Confederation, Congress was *unicameral* — meaning it had **only one legislative chamber**. Each state, large or small, had one vote, and there was **no separate Senate or House of Representatives**.

The Constitution changed that by creating a *bicameral* legislature — two houses — to balance the voices of the people and the states. This "Great Compromise" became the foundation for the U.S. Congress we know today.

Patriot's Reflection

When the Articles of Confederation began to fail, America faced its first great test of endurance. Freedom had been won — but freedom alone could not feed soldiers, pay debts, or settle disputes between the states.

The men who had fought together for liberty now struggled to govern together in peace. Each state guarded its power, and the nation drifted without direction. The dream of unity — the very purpose of the Revolution — seemed to fade in the winds of independence.

Yet in that moment of weakness, the Founders began to understand something profound: liberty cannot last without order, and order cannot endure without shared purpose. The Articles had been written from fear of tyranny; what the nation needed now was faith in cooperation.

From the lessons of failure came the courage to begin again — to build something stronger, wiser, and freer. The call for change would soon echo across the colonies, summoning the same patriots who had once pledged their lives for independence. Their next mission would not be to fight a war, but to **forge a union.**

Chapter 3 – The Birth of the Constitution

The Framework of a Republic

"We the People of the United States, in Order to form a more perfect Union…"
— *The Constitution of the United States, 1787*

 Freedom Fact

The Constitution was not written overnight — it was *forged* in debate, sweat, and compromise. From May to September 1787, delegates from twelve states gathered in Philadelphia to fix a broken government. Instead, they built something entirely new: a system that balanced freedom with order.

A Brief Story

By 1787, the young republic was drifting. The Articles of Confederation had proven too weak — Congress could not tax, enforce laws, or even pay soldiers. Shays' Rebellion had frightened many leaders; anarchy seemed a real possibility.

So, on a warm spring morning, delegates arrived at the Pennsylvania State House — the same hall where they had declared independence eleven years earlier. Their mission: *revise* the Articles. But the moment George Washington entered the room, everything changed.

The tall Virginian had hoped to live out his days quietly at Mount Vernon. Yet when the delegates saw him, they rose in silence. Without objection, he was elected **President of the Convention.** He did not protest. He simply walked to the front, placed his hand upon the table, and called the assembly to order.

Windows were nailed shut to keep debates secret. The air grew hot and stale, the mood alternated between optimism and fury. Should they amend the old Articles or craft an entirely new plan? Large states demanded population-based representation; small states feared domination. Each side saw its survival at stake. The arguments thundered through the hall until at last Washington, usually calm and deliberate, struck the table with his hand and declared:

"Gentlemen, we must compromise!"

Out of that single word — *compromise* — came a miracle. Roger Sherman's "Great Compromise" created a Congress with two houses: one representing the people (the House of Representatives) and one representing the states (the Senate). At last, order began to take shape.

For four grueling months they argued, drafted, and revised. Outside, the city sweltered in the summer heat; inside, tempers flared, friendships strained, and faith was tested. Yet through exhaustion and doubt, reason slowly prevailed. James Madison — the quiet scholar from Virginia — became known as the *Father of the Constitution* for his detailed notes and tireless reasoning. Benjamin Franklin, then 81, offered humor and humility when tempers flared, reminding them that *"we must, indeed, all hang together, or most assuredly, we shall all hang separately."*

Finally, on September 17, 1787, thirty-nine delegates signed the finished document. The ink was barely dry, yet they knew its words would outlive them all. It began with three simple words that forever changed the course of history: **We the People**.

🧠 Trivia Time

1 **Where did the Constitutional Convention take place?**
Answer: Independence Hall (Pennsylvania State House) in Philadelphia.

2 **Who presided over the Convention?**
Answer: George Washington.

3 **How long did the Convention last?**
Answer: From May 25 to September 17, 1787 — nearly four months.

4 **How many delegates signed the Constitution?**
Answer: Thirty-nine out of fifty-five present.

5 **Who is known as the "Father of the Constitution"?**
Answer: James Madison.

6 **What two-house solution was called the "Great Compromise"?**
Answer: A bicameral legislature — House by population, Senate by equal state votes.

7 **Which delegate was 81 years old and offered humor and wisdom through the debates?**
Answer: Benjamin Franklin.

8 **What was the original purpose of the Convention?**
Answer: To revise the Articles of Confederation — but they ended up writing a new Constitution.

9 **On what date was the Constitution signed?**
Answer: September 17, 1787 — now celebrated as Constitution Day.

10 **What had to happen before the Constitution could take effect?**
Answer: It had to be ratified by nine of the thirteen states.

A Moment to Reflect

The Founders faced an impossible task: create a government strong enough to govern, but limited enough to stay free.
They feared tyranny as much as anarchy. Every word they wrote was weighed against the memory of kings and war.

Imagine yourself in that stifling room. Would you argue for power to the people or power to the states? Could you sign your name to a document no nation had ever seen before?

Challenge Corner

In the summer heat of 1787, delegates debated representation.
Should each state — large or small — have an equal vote?
Or should population decide power?

What do you think was fairer? Equality among states or equality among citizens?
If you had been in that room, how would you have voted?
Write your thoughts in your journal — and remember, compromise built a nation.

Did You Know?

The Constitution we read today was not written in peaceful certainty — it was forged in secrecy, tension, and intense debate. Delegates locked the doors of Independence Hall, swore an oath of confidentiality, and worked behind shuttered windows in the heat of a Philadelphia summer. They believed honesty required privacy, not publicity.

Most of the delegates expected only minor revisions to the Articles of Confederation. Instead, they ended up creating an entirely new form of government. George Washington sat silently in the president's chair, guiding the room without a single speech, while men like Madison, Hamilton, and Gouverneur Morris battled over every clause, comma, and idea.

Many compromises were hard-won. The Great Compromise blended large and small state interests; the Three-Fifths Compromise exposed the deep moral conflict of slavery; and debates over the executive nearly tore the room apart. At one point, Benjamin Franklin suggested that the delegates pray each morning — but surprisingly, the motion failed.

And yet, despite all the disagreements, the delegates signed their names to a document they knew wasn't perfect — but was strong enough to survive. Franklin famously remarked, while pointing at the carved sun on Washington's chair, that he had long wondered whether it was a rising sun or a setting sun.

On the final day, he said he believed it was a **rising** one.

 Freedom Fact:
The Constitution wasn't born out of unity — it was born out of disagreement, compromise, and courage. Its strength comes not from perfection, but from the willingness of imperfect people to pursue a more perfect Union.

🔥 Freedom Reflection

The Constitution's first three Articles are more than sections of law — they're a statement of priorities.
The Founders placed the Legislative Branch first because lawmaking begins with the people. Under the Articles of Confederation, there had been no president or federal court — only a Congress. The framers kept that spirit of representation at the heart of the new Republic, but refined it with balance and structure.

Article I – The Legislative Branch: Power begins here, because it flows from the consent of the governed. The people's representatives make the laws.

Article II – The Executive Branch: Power is carried out here. The President enforces the laws but is bound by them — a servant, not a ruler.

Article III – The Judicial Branch: Power is interpreted here. The courts ensure that laws remain faithful to the Constitution itself.

This order wasn't accidental — it was deliberate. The framers believed that freedom depends on law, and law must begin with the people. That is why the Constitution does not start with a president, or even a court, but with:

"All legislative Powers herein granted shall be vested in a Congress of the United States."

By placing the people's branch first, the framers declared that America would never be ruled from above, but governed from within. The Executive and Judicial branches exist to serve and safeguard the will of the people — not to replace it.

In a time when many schools no longer teach civics, understanding this order is understanding America itself. It reminds us that the Constitution is not a hierarchy of rulers, but a sequence of responsibilities — each accountable to the one before it, and all accountable to the people.

Freedom, they knew, could survive tyranny or turmoil — but not ignorance. That's why the first article belongs to us.

Tidbits about The Constitution

1. *It Was Written by Hand*
Jacob Shallus, assistant clerk of the Pennsylvania General Assembly, penned the final document on four large parchment sheets.

Freedom Fact: He was paid just $30 for the task — about $900 today.

2. *It Starts with the People*
The Preamble declares that the Constitution's power comes from the people themselves.

Reflection: This was revolutionary — no kings, no lords, only citizens governing citizens.

3. *A Living Framework*
Unlike the Articles, the Constitution included a process for amendments — so future generations could adapt without revolution.

Freedom Fact: The Founders wrote a system built to evolve, not to collapse.

4. *The Preamble Has Only 52 Words*
Yet those 52 words define the nation's purpose: unity, justice, tranquility, defense, welfare, and liberty.

Trivia Question: Q: How many objectives are listed in the Preamble? A: Six.

5. *It Required Compromise*
Large states won representation by population in the House; small states won equal representation in the Senate.

Reflection: The Constitution itself is a document of balance — between freedom and order, people and states.

6. *Three Branches for Balance*
The framers divided power among Legislative, Executive, and Judicial branches to prevent any from ruling alone.

Freedom Fact: Each branch mirrors a human virtue — reason (law), will (action), and judgment (truth).

7. *Ratification Was a Battle*
Nine states had to approve before the Constitution took effect. Federalists and Anti-Federalists clashed in newspapers and taverns over its meaning.

Reflection: Freedom thrives on debate — disagreement can be the first sign of a healthy republic.

8. *The Bill of Rights Was a Promise*
To win ratification, the framers pledged to add amendments protecting individual liberties.

Freedom Fact: Those ten amendments were added in 1791 — only four years later.

9. *Rhode Island Came Late to the Party*
The state that boycotted the Convention was the last to ratify — in May 1790.

Trivia Question: Q: Which state ratified the Constitution last? A: Rhode Island.

10. *It Inspired the World*
The U.S. Constitution became a model for over 150 nations.

Reflection: Its genius lies not in power, but in restraint — a government strong enough to protect freedom but limited enough to preserve it.

The Ink Well

The Constitution was not written in a single day.
It was shaped through long hours, hard arguments, and heated compromise.
Every word was weighed, debated, and placed with purpose —
because the Founders knew this would not be just a document for their time, but a guide for all time.

———————— ▪ ————————

They wrote not for kings or courts, but for citizens.
And they knew that freedom without structure would one day collapse under its own weight.

Take a moment to reflect:
What would you have argued for in that room?
What principles would you have refused to yield?

🦅 Patriot's Reflection

When the delegates signed the Constitution, they knew it was imperfect — but they believed that a nation guided by reason and faith could perfect it over time.

Franklin was asked what form of government they had created. He replied, "A Republic — if you can keep it."

That challenge still stands. The Constitution isn't just a document to read — it's a promise to uphold. Every generation must decide whether it will preserve the balance of liberty and order the Founders fought to define.

For more than two centuries, that balance has been tested — by war, by division, and by doubt. Yet each time, Americans have returned to the same foundation: a belief that freedom endures only when the people themselves are willing to defend it, debate it, and live by it.

It's vital to remember that our Republic is *not* a pure democracy. In a democracy, majority rules — even when the majority is wrong. In a Republic, the rule of law protects the rights of every individual, ensuring that liberty cannot be voted away by passion or popularity. A Republic places principle above impulse, reason above rage, and duty above comfort.

Freedom Fact:

The United States is a *Republic*, not a pure democracy. A Republic is a government of laws — not of men — where the majority cannot vote away the rights of the few.

Chapter 4 – Article I: The Legislative Branch

"The Voice of the People"

"All legislative Powers herein granted shall be vested in a Congress of the United States…"
— *The Constitution of the United States, Article I, Section 1*

Freedom Fact

Before America had a President or a Supreme Court, it had a Congress. The framers placed the legislative branch first in the Constitution because they believed that government must begin — and be held accountable — to the people's representatives.

Here, law is born not in palaces or courts, but through debate, compromise, and the consent of the governed. The Founders understood that true liberty depends not on a single ruler's wisdom, but on the collective voice of free citizens working through reason and representation.

The Articles of Confederation had already proven what happens when that balance fails — when there is no power to act, no structure to decide. So the framers designed Congress to be both strong and restrained, energetic but answerable to the people.

Every law, every debate, every vote in Congress still echoes that founding idea: that sovereignty rests not with kings or cabinets, but with the people themselves. Article I is the heartbeat of self-government — the place where liberty takes its first breath and its last defense.

🪶 A Brief Story

In the spring of **1789,** as the new Constitution came to life, members of the First Congress gathered in New York City's **Federal Hall,** a modest stone building overlooking Broad Street.
Forty-eight representatives arrived from eleven states — farmers, lawyers, merchants, veterans, and ministers — unsure if this new Republic would hold.

The air buzzed with questions:
How would laws be made?
Who would speak for whom?
Could a Congress of states truly serve a nation of people?

At the center of that debate was **James Madison,** the scholar from Virginia whose ideas had helped shape the Constitution itself. Madison argued that the people's voice must begin in the **House of Representatives,** directly elected every two years. But he also knew that passion needed patience — and so the **Senate** was born, a chamber where experience, wisdom, and state sovereignty could balance the will of the majority.

Outside, carriages rattled over cobblestones as citizens gathered to glimpse the dawn of a new government. Some whispered doubts; others prayed in gratitude. The sound of church bells mingled with shouts from the marketplace, a chorus of hope and uncertainty. Inside, beneath the tall windows and flickering candlelight, quills scratched across parchment as the foundation of American law took shape — one clause, one vote, one argument at a time.

Each man in that chamber knew the world was watching. They had seen revolution, endured chaos, and now faced the burden of peace. The air carried more than the scent of ink and candle wax — it carried the weight of promise. What they built would decide whether liberty could govern itself — not by force of arms, but by the discipline of law and the consent of free men.
And as the day faded, those weary delegates could not have known that their words would echo through centuries, calling each generation to defend what they began.

📜 Trivia Time

1 **Who presides over the House of Representatives?**
Answer: The Speaker of the House.

2 **How many senators does each state have?**
Answer: Two.

3 **How long is a senator's term?**
Answer: Six years.

4 **What is the minimum age to serve in the House?**
Answer: Twenty-five.

5 **Which chamber introduces bills for raising revenue?**
Answer: The House of Representatives.

6 **Who breaks a tie vote in the Senate?**
Answer: The Vice President — who also serves as the President of the Senate.

7 **What fraction of both houses must approve to override a presidential veto?**
Answer: Two-thirds.

8 **How often must Congress meet each year?**
Answer: At least once.

9 **In what city did the first U.S. Congress convene under the Constitution?**
Answer: New York City.

10 **What must happen before a bill becomes law?**
Answer: It must pass both the House and Senate and be signed by the President — or passed again by two-thirds if vetoed.

A Moment to Reflect

The framers built Congress to be a mirror of the people — but no mirror is perfect. Imagine sitting in that first chamber in Federal Hall in 1789, listening to voices from every corner of the new nation. The air hums with ideas — liberty, law, taxes, trade — all colliding in one room. Would you be patient enough to listen to every side? Or would you want to act quickly, to see progress now?
The Founders believed that the slow rhythm of debate was not weakness, but wisdom. True freedom, they knew, must be argued for again and again.

Challenge Corner

The framers faced a hard question: Should laws be decided by population or by state?
Large states demanded representation by people; small states insisted on equality among states.
Their answer — the Great Compromise — created the House and Senate, balancing passion with patience.
If you were there, how would you have chosen? One vote per state, or one vote per person?
Write your thoughts in your journal or the ink well. What kind of fairness keeps freedom alive?

Did You Know?

The framers feared both tyranny and stagnation. To prevent either, they split the legislative branch into two chambers.
One — the **House of Representatives** — would move with the people's passions.
The other — the **Senate** — would temper those passions with reason and restraint.
Together, they created a system that could act boldly when needed and pause wisely when patience was required.

This balance — of people and states, energy and stability — became known as the **Great Compromise**, and it remains one of the most brilliant features of the American system.

⊘ Freedom Reflection – The People's Power

Article I reminds us that government begins where liberty lives — with the people.
Every law written in Congress carries the echo of that first declaration: that power is *lent*, not owned.
Our Founders knew that when the people stop watching, representation turns to rule.

That's why they built a system of transparency and accountability — debates recorded, votes counted, and laws published for every citizen to read.
They believed that an informed people would guard their own liberty better than any ruler ever could.

Congress is not the government's voice — it is ours.
And when it forgets that truth, it is the duty of free citizens to remind it.

Tidbits from Article I

1. The Meaning of "Legislative Powers"

To *legislate* means "to make laws." But the Founders went further —
they defined not only who makes the law, but how.
Congress cannot simply *declare* its will; it must act through open debate,
recorded votes, and accountability to the electorate.

> **Freedom Fact:** Lawmaking is not an act of authority — it's an act
> of consent.

2. What Does "Bicameral" Mean?

The Constitution created a **bicameral** legislature — two chambers —
the House and the Senate.
Each chamber has distinct powers and responsibilities, but both must
agree for a law to pass.
This design ensures that no single majority, no matter how loud or large,
can rule without restraint.

> *Definition Reminder:* The Articles of Confederation had a
> **unicameral** Congress — just one chamber, where every state had one
> vote.

3. Terms, Ages, and Balance

Representatives serve for two years, senators for six.
This means the House is constantly renewed, while the Senate provides
stability.
It's the difference between the wind of change and the anchor of
wisdom — and the Republic needs both to stay upright.

🏛 4. The House: The People's Chamber

The House was designed to mirror the nation's heartbeat.
Every two years, voters decide who speaks for them — keeping
representatives close to their will.
That's why tax and spending bills begin there: because they come
directly from the pockets of the people.

🕊 5. The Senate: The States' Voice

Originally, senators were chosen by state legislatures, not by direct vote.
This gave the states themselves a seat at the federal table.
Only after the 17th Amendment (1913) did citizens elect senators
directly.
Even then, the Senate retained its slower pace, longer terms, and
deliberative character — a place where policy is meant to cool before
becoming law.

💥 6. Powers and Limits

Congress can declare war, coin money, establish courts, and regulate
trade.
But for every power granted, there's a limit written beside it — a
reminder that authority exists only by permission of the governed.

🏛 7. The Elastic Clause

Article I, Section 8 ends with the **Necessary and Proper Clause**, often
called the *Elastic Clause*.
It gives Congress flexibility to carry out its powers as the nation grows
— but also opens the door to debate over what "necessary" really
means.
Every generation must decide how far that elastic should stretch before
it snaps.

🚩 8. Checks and Balances in Action

Congress passes laws, but the president can veto them.
The courts interpret laws, but Congress can limit jurisdiction or amend
legislation.

Each branch can restrain the others — like gears in motion, friction prevents runaway power.

 ### 9. The People's Purse

Article I grants Congress the **power of the purse** — control over taxation and spending.
No money leaves the Treasury without its consent.
It's one of the most powerful tools for accountability, ensuring that government cannot act without the people's financial permission.

 ### 10. The Spirit of Deliberation

The Founders knew that speed is the enemy of wisdom.
By design, Congress moves slowly, forcing patience, debate, and compromise.
It's not a flaw — it's a feature.
They built a system that protects liberty from haste and guards truth from impulse.

Freedom Challenge

Imagine Congress in session — debate fills the chamber, voices rise and fall, and votes divide along narrow lines. In that noise lies the sound of freedom: disagreement without destruction. But today, too often, compromise is mistaken for weakness. The Founders knew better.

They built a system meant to argue, to pause, and to seek common ground for the common good. Your challenge is to look at our nation's divisions and ask yourself: *Where could reason speak louder than anger?* Write how you would bring balance between conviction and cooperation — because the Republic survives only when its citizens practice the art of debate with the grace of respect.

The Ink Well

The Constitution gives Congress the power to make laws — but also the duty to restrain itself.
When power grows too quickly, liberty shrinks just as fast.

———————— ▮ ————————

If you had stood in Federal Hall in 1789, what law would you have proposed first for this new nation?

What principle would you have defended above all others?
Use this space to write, reflect, and remind yourself that every generation writes its own chapter in the American story.

🦅 Patriot's Reflection

The legislative branch was designed to be noisy, divided, and slow — because freedom deserves careful deliberation. The Founders had lived under governments where laws came swiftly from a distant throne, without consent and without recourse. They knew that unity without debate is not strength but submission, and that silence in the halls of government is often the first warning sign of tyranny.

Congress was meant to be the people's voice — loud, imperfect, courageous, and unafraid to argue. Every amendment offered, every vote cast, every hour spent in debate is the sound of liberty at work. It reminds us that disagreement is not a threat to the Republic but a safeguard of it. A nation where citizens fall quiet, where laws pass without scrutiny, or where representatives stop answering to the people, is a nation dangerously close to forgetting its foundation.

When Congress listens, the Republic breathes. When it drifts from the people's will, freedom does not fall with a crash — it fades slowly, quietly, in the spaces where citizens stop watching and leaders stop remembering who they serve. The Founders built Article I to prevent that drift, to anchor power to accountability and bind authority to transparency.

In a free nation, the people do not wait for permission to be heard. They write, speak, vote, challenge, and remind their representatives that public office is stewardship, not ownership. The health of the Republic has always depended on citizens who remain engaged, informed, and willing to demand better when Congress forgets its purpose.

The question remains, just as Franklin posed it on that hot Philadelphia afternoon:
"You have a Republic... if you can keep it."
The keeping of it is not Congress's duty alone — it belongs to every American who understands that liberty survives only when the people continue to guide, question, and guard those who govern in their name.

Chapter 5 – Article II: The Executive Branch

"The Weight of the Oath"

"The executive Power shall be vested in a President of the United States of America…"
— *The Constitution of the United States, Article II, Section 1*

⚖️ Freedom Fact

Before there was a president, there was a fear — fear of kings, of tyranny, of a single man wielding unchecked power.
Yet the framers also knew a nation cannot govern itself without leadership. So they designed a new kind of executive — one bound by duty, answerable to law, and chosen not by mobs or monarchs, but through a careful balance of people and states.

That balance became the **Electoral College** — a uniquely American safeguard ensuring that every state, large or small, has a voice in choosing the president. It prevents a few crowded cities from drowning out the heartland, preserving the principle that *we are a Union of states as well as citizens.*

In time, the **12th Amendment** refined this process, separating the votes for president and vice president to strengthen the clarity and fairness of the system.
It stands today as a testament to the Founders' wisdom — that liberty survives not through speed, but through structure.

A Brief Story

April 30, 1789 — a cool morning in New York City.
Crowds pressed into the streets, climbing fences and windowsills to catch a glimpse of the tall Virginian in a plain brown suit. Church bells rang across the harbor, ships fired salutes, and from every balcony hung the new nation's flag — thirteen stars stitched in a hopeful circle.

Just weeks earlier, every state legislature had cast its votes for president under the new Constitution. The results were unanimous — all sixty-nine electors chose **George Washington.**

That method of choosing him — through the Electoral College — had been born from the same tension that nearly tore the Convention apart. In Philadelphia, the delegates from Virginia, representing the larger states, demanded that the presidency be decided by simple majority. But Rhode Island's delegate rose in protest, warning that small states would never again have a voice in choosing their leader. The room fell into argument — voices clashing over fairness, power, and representation. It was a battle of principle, not pride.

When tempers boiled, it was Washington himself who quieted the chamber. The compromise that followed preserved both equality among citizens and sovereignty among states. The Electoral College became their solution — a system that gave every state a say, large or small, and ensured that no single region could command the Republic.

That humility was his strength. It was the very reason the people trusted him with so much power.

On the balcony of Federal Hall, he placed his hand on a worn family Bible and swore the first oath of office:

"I do solemnly swear that I will faithfully execute the Office of President of the United States, and will to the best of my Ability, preserve, protect, and defend the Constitution of the United States."

The air filled with cheers, the roll of drums, and the thunder of cannon fire echoing off the bay. Yet Washington's face remained solemn. He knew that every act, every decision, would set a precedent — and that *power, once unleashed, rarely returns to its leash.*

He paused, bowed his head, and whispered a silent prayer — that Providence might guide the Republic better than any man could. The world was watching: kings, ministers, and commoners alike. And in that moment, a new experiment in liberty took its first breath.

He meant to show the world that the presidency would be one of **service, not sovereignty.**

In the years that followed, his steady hand guided the infant Republic through rebellion and unrest. When farmers in western Pennsylvania rose in protest over the whiskey tax, Washington could have crushed them from afar. Instead, he mounted his horse, donned his uniform, and rode at the head of the militia — not as a conqueror, but as a citizen enforcing the law he himself obeyed.

He had been chosen by the people, confirmed by the states, and bound by conscience. He proved that strength could wear the face of restraint — and that a leader's greatest weapon is example.

Trivia Time

1 **Who was the first President of the United States?**
Answer: George Washington.

2 **What year did the first presidential inauguration take place?**
Answer: 1789.

3 **How long is a presidential term?**
Answer: Four years.

4 **What amendment refined the presidential election process?**
Answer: The Twelfth Amendment (ratified in 1804).

5 **Who administers the presidential oath of office?**
Answer: The Chief Justice of the United States.

6 **Who is Commander-in-Chief of the armed forces?**
Answer: The President.

7 **Which president set the two-term precedent?**
Answer: George Washington.

8 **What event tested the authority of the new executive branch?**
Answer: The Whiskey Rebellion (1794).

9 **What is the President's primary duty under the Constitution?**
Answer: To "preserve, protect, and defend the Constitution of the United States."

10 **How is the President of the United States officially chosen?**
Answer: By the Electoral College — ensuring all states, large and small, have a voice in the nation's highest office.

A Moment to Reflect

George Washington never wanted to be a king — and yet, the nation he helped create needed a leader. Imagine the weight he carried as he stood on the balcony of Federal Hall, one hand on the Bible, the other raised to heaven. No president had ever taken that oath before. Every step he took would define what "Mr. President" meant.

Would you have had the humility to lead without seeking power? Could you shoulder authority without letting it rule you?

The presidency, Washington believed, was not a prize — it was a trust. A sacred promise to lead with restraint so that the people would never again live under a crown.

Challenge Corner

When the Founders designed the presidency, they argued for weeks about how a single person could hold power without becoming a tyrant. Some feared a strong executive; others feared a weak one. Their solution — the checks and balances of Article II — remains one of the Constitution's boldest ideas.

If you were in that debate, would you have argued for more power or less? Should a president act quickly in crisis, or wait for Congress to decide?

Think about your own definition of leadership. Does real strength come from command — or from character?

Did You Know?

When the framers created the presidency, they feared two extremes — a weak leader who could not act, and a strong one who would not stop acting. Their solution was genius: a single executive, accountable to both the law and the people, balanced by checks from the other branches.

Even the title *"President"* was chosen with care. Rejecting "Your Excellency" or "Your Majesty," Washington insisted on simplicity — *Mr. President* — a reminder that the office was one of service, not sovereignty.

The **Electoral College** became part of this careful design. It ensured that all states — not just the most populous — would have a say in choosing the nation's leader. Without it, the will of a few cities could eclipse entire regions. By blending popular vote with state representation, the framers preserved both equality among citizens and fairness among states.

Here's how it works — and why it still matters:

1 The People Vote Within Their States.

Every four years, citizens cast their ballots for president. Their votes decide *which slate of electors* (chosen beforehand by each political party) will represent their state. This means the *majority vote* happens **inside each state**, not across the nation as a whole. The system keeps the contest fair between large and small states, ensuring that no single region dominates the rest.

2 The Electors Cast the Official Votes.

Those electors — one for each senator and representative — meet in their state capitals to cast the official votes for president and vice president. They are not members of Congress or federal officials; they are citizens entrusted to reflect their state's choice. Their votes are then certified and counted before a joint session of Congress, completing the constitutional process.

When confusion and partisan rivalry marred the election of 1800, the **Twelfth Amendment** brought clarity. It required separate ballots for president and vice president — a safeguard that strengthened both the system's transparency and its legitimacy.

Far from being outdated, the Electoral College remains one of the most brilliant safeguards of the American Republic. It protects every state's voice, prevents domination by a national majority, and preserves the balance between *the people* and *the union of states* that defines who we are.

The presidency, then and now, is not a throne — it is a trust.
Its power depends on character more than command, and it succeeds only when guided by conscience.

Freedom Fact:

The President and Vice President are the *only* federal officials chosen through the Electoral College.
Every other elected position — from members of Congress to state governors and local officials — is decided by **direct popular vote** within their states or districts.

This design was intentional. The Founders believed that a single national office — representing *all* the people and *all* the states — required a process that reflected the entire Union, not just population centers.

 It's a reminder that America is both a *Republic of citizens* and a *Union of states* — each voice distinct, yet bound together in the same great experiment of self-government.

Freedom Reflection – The Power of Restraint

The measure of leadership is not how much power one holds, but how little one needs to use it.
Washington showed that true strength lies in restraint — in the courage to act with reason when others demand reaction.

Every president since has stood in his shadow, weighed by the same standard: will they serve the Constitution, or themselves?
The oath binds them not to victory, but to virtue. It reminds us that freedom's greatest guardian is not might, but morality.

When power listens to conscience, liberty endures.
When it does not, the Republic begins to tremble.

Tidbits from Article II

 ### 1. The President's Oath

The oath of office appears word for word in the Constitution — a promise of loyalty to law, not to power.
The Founders and members of the First Congress, mindful of the monarchies they had just escaped, wanted to ensure that no American leader would ever swear allegiance to a person, a party, or even a branch of government — only to the Constitution itself.
It was their way of binding ambition to accountability.

 ### Freedom Fact:

It's the only oath specifically written into the document itself — a reminder that the presidency begins not with privilege, but with a pledge.

 ### 2. Commander-in-Chief

The President commands the military, but only Congress can declare war — a balance designed to prevent one man from wielding the sword of the Republic alone.

Still, the Founders understood that liberty must be protected not just by law, but by readiness.
In moments of crisis, when the nation faces sudden attack or imminent danger, the President may act swiftly to defend the Republic — deploying forces, securing borders, or ordering immediate measures of protection.

This power does not replace Congress — it buys time for Congress to debate, authorize, and fund broader action. It allows the executive to fulfill his oath: *to preserve, protect, and defend the Constitution of the United States.*

Freedom Fact:

This balance between action and accountability ensures that the President can move quickly when seconds matter — yet must always answer to the people once the smoke clears..

3. Appointments and Treaties

The President nominates judges, ambassadors, and officers, but the Senate must confirm them. It's another reminder that trust must be shared, not assumed.

 ### 4. The Power to Veto

The veto lets the President check Congress, but Congress can override it with a two-thirds vote — proof that even the highest office bows to the people's will.

 ### 5. Impeachment

If a President abuses power, the House can impeach, and the Senate can remove. It's not a political tool — it's a safeguard of the Republic.

 ### 6. Peaceful Transfer of Power

Every inauguration, every oath, every handshake between outgoing and incoming leaders, renews the covenant of the Republic — that power changes hands without bloodshed.

 ### 7. The Cabinet

Washington formed the first Cabinet — four men who advised, debated, and sometimes defied him. It was his way of ensuring no single voice, not even his own, went unchallenged.

 ### 8. Term Limits

Washington served two terms, then voluntarily stepped aside — setting the unwritten rule that lasted until the 22nd Amendment made it law in 1951.

 ### 9. Faith and Providence

Washington often spoke of Divine Providence guiding the nation's path. His faith wasn't in his own wisdom, but in the enduring wisdom of liberty itself.

10. Legacy of Example

Washington left behind no crown, no heirs, and no dynasty — only the example of a man who proved that the highest power of all is self-restraint.

⚙ Freedom Reflection

The Founders gave the President power enough to act — but bound him to the Constitution so that he must always act within it. Today, every agency that serves the nation — from the military and Department of Justice to the FBI, CIA, and every three-letter branch of enforcement — traces its authority to Article II and, through it, to the people. The President stands as the head of this vast system, not as a ruler, but as a steward — the ultimate officer responsible for ensuring that every department serves the public good and obeys the law.

Congress oversees, advises, and holds hearings — but the power to lead, to direct, and to correct these agencies rests with the Executive. That responsibility is enormous, and it demands both strength and moral clarity. For when the agencies of government forget their purpose, it is the President's duty to remind them who they serve — and to act when they do not.

☞ Reflection Thought:

The Founders feared kings, not leaders. They designed a presidency strong enough to defend freedom, but accountable enough to never destroy it. The buck stops at the President's desk — but so does the duty to defend liberty itself."

The Ink Well

Leadership is tested not by crisis, but by character.
If you were president, how would you balance strength with humility?
What principle would you never compromise, even when the world demanded it?

🦅 Patriot's Reflection

The Executive Branch reminds us that freedom endures only when power is guided by virtue. Washington's presidency proved that law and leadership can coexist — that strength and humility are not opposites but allies. He understood that authority must never be used to elevate the leader, but to uphold the people who entrusted him with it. In every decision he made, he sought not applause, but accountability.

He showed the Republic that it needs neither kings nor tyrants, but citizens willing to shoulder the weight of duty with grace. His example became the quiet standard by which every president has been measured — a reminder that character is the first qualification for power in a free nation.

Every president who takes the oath joins a chain that began on that cool morning in 1789. Some would face war, others economic trials, and still others the divisions of a changing nation. But each must confront the same question: will they preserve the Republic, or merely preside over it? Will they use the authority of their office to protect the Constitution — or themselves?

Their authority may differ, but their responsibility has never changed: to safeguard liberty, not their legacy. The presidency is not a stage for ambition or a throne for admiration. It is a trust — temporary, solemn, and rooted in the will of the governed.

For in the end, the presidency is not about the man who leads — it is about the people who remain free enough to choose him, challenge him, and hold him to the oath he swore. As long as the nation remembers that truth, the Executive Branch will remain not a threat to liberty, but one of its greatest guardians.

Chapter 6 – Article III: The Judicial Branch

"The Guardian of the Constitution"

"The judicial Power of the United States, shall be vested in one supreme Court, and in such inferior Courts as the Congress may from time to time ordain and establish."
— *The Constitution of the United States, Article III, Section 1*

 Freedom Fact

Before America had marble courtrooms or famous opinions, it had an idea — that no man or office should stand above the law.
The Founders feared not only kings, but also the tyranny of temporary majorities — the moment when passion outruns principle. So they created a branch that would speak softly but carry great weight: the Judiciary.

Article III gave the nation a system of courts to interpret the laws, not to write or enforce them. Its strength lies in its restraint — in judging only when asked, and ruling only according to the Constitution.
The Judicial Branch exists to steady the other two — keeping ambition in check and liberty in balance.

A Brief Story

In the spring of **1789**, as the new government took shape, Congress passed the **Judiciary Act**, establishing a Supreme Court and lower federal courts. The first justices — six men appointed by President George Washington — met in a borrowed chamber in New York City. There were no black robes, no gavels, no grandeur. Only a wooden table, quills in ink wells, and a belief that law could guide freedom better than force.

At first, their cases were few. They spent much of their time "riding circuit" — traveling by horseback to hear disputes in towns across the states. It was humble work for a high court, but it grounded the new nation's justice system in the daily lives of its people.

Then came **1803**. The young Republic found itself divided over politics and power. When a case called *Marbury v. Madison* reached the Court, Chief Justice **John Marshall** saw an opportunity — and a duty. In his opinion, he declared:

"It is emphatically the province and duty of the Judicial Department to say what the law is."

With those words, the Court claimed the power of **judicial review** — the right to strike down laws that violated the Constitution. No army enforced that power, no crowd demanded it. Yet it changed everything. From that moment on, the Constitution stood above every branch, every law, and every leader.

This was not a grab for power — it was the birth of balance.

🧠 Trivia Time

1 Who was the first Chief Justice of the United States?
Answer: John Jay.

2 What law created the federal court system?
Answer: The Judiciary Act of 1789.

3 What landmark case established the power of judicial review?
Answer: Marbury v. Madison (1803).

4 How many justices currently serve on the Supreme Court?
Answer: Nine.

5 How long do federal judges serve?
Answer: For life, during "good behavior."

6 Who nominates federal judges?
Answer: The President, with Senate confirmation.

7 What does the Supreme Court's motto read above its doors?
Answer: "Equal Justice Under Law."

8 Where does the Supreme Court meet today?
Answer: In Washington, D.C., in a building completed in 1935.

9 What is the Supreme Court's highest duty?
Answer: To uphold the Constitution as the supreme law of the land.

10 What happens when a law conflicts with the Constitution?
Answer: The Supreme Court can strike it down, ensuring that no branch of government rises above the law.

A Moment to Reflect

The Founders gave the judiciary no armies, no treasury, and no voters — only the power of judgment.

Imagine standing in that quiet courtroom, where the clash of politics fades and only principle remains. The judge's robe is plain, but the responsibility it carries is immense: to measure every law against the Constitution itself.

Could you bear that burden — knowing your decision might shape the future of a nation?

Justice was never meant to follow opinion or favor; it was meant to follow truth. And sometimes, truth must stand alone.

Challenge Corner

In the early years of the Republic, the courts were seen as the weakest branch — yet today, they often have the final say in the nation's greatest debates.

Do you believe judges should interpret the Constitution exactly as it was written, or should they adapt its meaning to the times?

Imagine you were a justice faced with a difficult case where law and public opinion collide. Would you follow the crowd — or the Constitution?

Write your answer in your journal or the ink well. The strength of liberty often depends on a single voice that refuses to waver.

Did You Know?

The Founders wrestled with how to choose judges. Some wanted them elected by the people; others feared that politics would corrupt the bench. In the end, they chose appointment — with Senate confirmation — to safeguard independence from public passion.

Judges would not rule by opinion polls, but by principle. Their duty would be to the Constitution alone.

But over time, a flaw crept into the system. Because the **President nominates** justices and the **Senate confirms** them, politics has found its way into what was meant to be the most impartial branch of government.

Today, the balance of the Court can shift when one party controls both the White House and the Senate. Debates rise over nominations, and calls echo to "expand" or "reshape" the Court whenever one side feels outnumbered.

The Founders never intended the Supreme Court to be an arm of any party. They designed it to stand apart — to judge the law, not to join the argument.

When partisanship invades the bench, justice begins to lean. And when justice leans, the Republic tilts with it.

Yet the solution is not more judges, but better judgment.

For the Court's true strength has never been in its size — it's in its integrity.

The legislative and executive branches move with the people's will, but the judicial branch exists to preserve their rights when the majority forgets them. It's the quiet hand that turns chaos into order without force.

Throughout history, the Court has stood in moments of great trial — slavery, segregation, free speech, and civil rights. Not every decision was perfect, but each one became part of the nation's long journey toward a more perfect Union.

When the Court gets it right, it reminds us that laws can bend toward justice without breaking the Republic.

Freedom Reflection – The Scales of Liberty

Laws can command obedience, but they cannot command conscience. That is why justice must be blind — not to truth, but to prejudice.

Every law passed by Congress and every order signed by the President must meet its final test before a judge. In that courtroom, power must yield to principle. A farmer and a president stand equal before the same law, under the same flag.

The Founders expected that decisions of the Supreme Court would stir anger in the halls of Congress and in the hearts of citizens — for wherever justice draws a line, someone stands on the other side of it. But they never intended that disagreement become destruction. Today, when rulings bring outrage or even threats against those who serve on the bench, we are reminded that liberty depends not on passion, but on principle.

To remain free, we must defend the independence of those who interpret the law — even when we dislike their judgment. That is the true test of a Republic.

"Textualism," the idea that judges should interpret the Constitution by its written words rather than by shifting moods or modern wishes, is not stubbornness — it is fidelity. The words were written to endure, not to drift with every tide of opinion.

When judges remain faithful to those words, they preserve the balance between liberty and authority. When they drift into politics, the balance falters — and freedom begins to lean.

The Founders did not give the courts armies or treasuries; they gave them words — the power of reason written in law. And for over two centuries, that quiet power has held the Republic together when passion threatened to tear it apart.

Tidbits from Article III

1. Life Tenure and Good Behavior

Federal judges serve for life, as long as they remain honorable. This protects them from political pressure and ensures their loyalty is to justice — not to popularity or party.

☞ **Freedom Fact:** Their job security isn't a privilege; it's a protection for every citizen, ensuring that no one's rights rise or fall with an election cycle.

2. Judicial Review

Though the Constitution never names it outright, the power to judge a law's constitutionality is the heart of Article III. It is how the courts keep Congress and the President bound to the same rulebook.

☞ **Freedom Fact:** Judicial review is not a sword — it's a shield.

3. Court Structure

Congress holds the authority to create and organize lower courts. This keeps the judiciary adaptable as the nation grows.

☞ **Freedom Fact:** The Supreme Court may be the highest court, but it is not the only one. Justice begins in local courts and climbs upward — just like the people's voices.

4. The First Supreme Court

In 1789, Congress established the first Supreme Court with six justices. They met in borrowed chambers and sometimes rode horseback from city to city to hear cases.

☞ **Freedom Fact:** The Court had no marble halls or grandeur at first — only a mission to interpret the law faithfully.

5. The Case of Marbury v. Madison (1803)

This case established the precedent of judicial review, affirming that the Supreme Court could strike down laws that violated the Constitution.

☞ **Freedom Fact:** Chief Justice John Marshall's decision in *Marbury v. Madison* turned Article III from words on paper into the guardian of the Republic.

6. Independence through Restraint

The Founders feared judges who acted like kings, but they also feared lawmakers who ignored the Constitution. The balance comes when judges interpret — not invent — law.

Freedom Fact: True independence is measured by self-restraint.

7. "One Supreme Court"

The Constitution names only one court by title — the Supreme Court — leaving all others to Congress. This shows that the Framers valued principle over structure.

Freedom Fact: The strength of the judiciary lies not in its size, but in its integrity.

8. The Right to Trial by Jury

Article III guarantees that every person accused of a crime has the right to a trial by jury. That safeguard places ordinary citizens inside the courtroom as defenders of liberty.

Freedom Fact: A jury is democracy in its purest form — neighbors judging facts, not power.

9. The Limits of Treason

The Constitution defines treason narrowly — waging war against the United States or aiding its enemies — and requires two witnesses to prove it.

Freedom Fact: The Founders knew that tyranny often begins by accusing opponents of treason; they wrote safeguards to stop it.

10. The People's Last Defense

The judiciary was meant to be the quiet branch — not seeking headlines or power, but standing guard when others fail.

Freedom Fact: When politics roars and passions rise, the courts remind us that in America, law — not anger — has the final word.

✎ The Ink Well

Justice wears no crown and takes no sides. It listens, weighs, and decides.

Take a moment to reflect:

———————— ⚱ ————————

How do judges protect freedom even when their decisions are unpopular?

Why is it important that every person — no matter their wealth or title — stands equal before the same law?

Use this space to write your thoughts, questions, or a principle you would defend if you sat on the bench of liberty.

🦅 Patriot's Reflection

"The courts must declare the sense of the law." — *Chief Justice John Marshall, 1803*

The Judicial Branch reminds us that freedom is not merely won — it is maintained. Laws may be written in ink, sometimes even by the stroke of a quill, but they live only through judgment. Each time a court upholds the Constitution, it renews the promise made in Philadelphia — that America would be a nation governed not by rulers, but by laws.

The Supreme Court may seem distant, yet its reach touches every citizen, every town, every choice. From the rights we speak to the justice we seek, its quiet decisions shape the daily rhythm of our Republic. For when justice speaks, the nation listens — and sometimes, it trembles.

The Founders built a government of action and balance: Congress makes the law, the President enforces it, and the Judiciary ensures it remains just. When these three walk in harmony, liberty stands tall — but when any one forgets its limits, the balance falters.

True justice requires courage — the courage to stand against pressure, politics, and pride. The Constitution endures only when those who interpret it do so with integrity and humility.

🕊 Freedom Reflection Thought:
The Constitution is only as strong as the conscience of those who interpret it. Judges, like citizens, must remember: the law is not power — it is a promise kept alive by courage.

Chapter 7 – Article IV: The States and the Union

"E Pluribus Unum — Out of Many, One."
Article IV of the Constitution

 Freedom Fact

When the ink dried on the Constitution, the thirteen states were still more like neighbors than family. Each had its own laws, currencies, and identities — bound together by history, but divided by habit. Article IV was written to mend those seams.

It declared that a Virginian and a New Yorker shared the same rights; that a judgment in Georgia must be honored in Massachusetts; that a citizen's liberty did not stop at a border. This was the promise of *union* — not by force, but by faith.

Through its "Full Faith and Credit" and "Privileges and Immunities" clauses, Article IV turned separate sovereignties into one people under a common standard of justice. It also charted the path for new states to join the Republic, proving that freedom was not a closed circle, but an ever-widening frontier.

The Founders knew that a republic divided by rivalry could not endure. So they built in both strength and flexibility — a system where the nation would protect the states, and the states would uphold the nation. Article IV is that handshake, written in ink by a quill: an agreement that the United States would remain exactly that — united.

A Brief Story

By the 1790s, the young Republic stretched from the Atlantic to the edge of the Appalachian Mountains. New lands beckoned, and settlers carried with them not just plows and rifles, but questions.
If they founded new communities, would those lands be states or territories? Would their laws match those of Virginia or Pennsylvania — or neither?

In 1787, even before the Constitution took effect, the Northwest Ordinance had planted the seed: new states would enter "on equal footing" with the old. Article IV gave that promise constitutional weight. Every star added to the flag would shine with the same sovereignty as the first thirteen.

But unity demanded trust. Some states resisted recognizing court rulings from others. Debates flared over fugitives, trade duties, and taxation. Each quarrel tested the idea that one Republic could bridge many governments. Yet, time and again, the Constitution held.

When Kentucky, Tennessee, and later Ohio joined the Union, they did so not as colonies of the East but as equal partners in the great American experiment. Every oath sworn, every law honored across borders, stitched another thread into the fabric of the nation.

In those formative years, the ink of the Founders' quills had barely dried, yet its power reached across mountains and rivers. That same ink — the promise of shared liberty — still binds fifty states today. From those early struggles came a truth that endures: America's strength lies not in uniformity, but in unity — a nation of fifty voices speaking through one Constitution.

🕐 Trivia Time

1 What does Article IV primarily deal with?
Answer: The relationship between the states and the federal government.

2 What clause requires states to honor each other's laws and records?
Answer: The Full Faith and Credit Clause.

3 What clause ensures citizens are treated equally in all states?
Answer: The Privileges and Immunities Clause.

4 Who approves the admission of new states?
Answer: Congress.

5 What promise does the Constitution make to every state?
Answer: A "Republican Form of Government" and protection against invasion or domestic violence.

6 Which law set the precedent for adding new states?
Answer: The Northwest Ordinance of 1787.

7 Can two states merge or divide without Congress's consent?
Answer: No.

8 Which article guarantees that state laws cannot contradict the Constitution?
Answer: The Supremacy Clause (Article VI) — but Article IV lays the groundwork.

9 What state was the first added to the Union after the original thirteen?
Answer: Vermont (1791).

10 What phrase on the Great Seal reflects the spirit of Article IV?
Answer: E Pluribus Unum — "Out of many, one."

A Moment to Reflect

Imagine you are a citizen in 1791 — a farmer in Kentucky or a tradesman in Vermont. The ink on your state's admission papers is still drying. Would you feel part of a new nation, or loyal only to your state? The Founders built Article IV to ensure that both loyalties could coexist — that pride in one's home would strengthen, not divide, the Union.

What binds us today? The same principle: that liberty must be shared to survive.

Challenge Corner

When states disagree — over trade, resources, or ideology — the test of unity begins again.
How should a free people balance state sovereignty with national strength? Should every state have the right to act entirely on its own, or must some laws bind all equally?
Write your answer. Would the Founders recognize today's balance as what they intended — or would they reach for their quills once more?

Did You Know?

The "Full Faith and Credit" clause was revolutionary for its time. No other confederation had ever demanded that one government recognize another's laws and judgments. It turned a patchwork of colonies into a single nation of citizens.

The Founders also foresaw expansion. They wanted new states to share equal power, not serve as territories forever beholden to the old ones. That principle of equality ensured that the Union could grow — from 13 states to 50 or more — without breaking its promise of balance.

☞ **Freedom Fact:** Every star on the flag represents not just a place on the map, but a covenant — a state that pledged its faith to the Union and, in return, received the protection of liberty.

🧭 Freedom Reflection – One Nation, Many Homes

Article IV turns neighbors into a nation. It says your rights don't stop at a border, your contracts don't expire at a river, and your citizenship doesn't shrink when you cross a state line. Unity here isn't sameness—it's promise: that fifty different places can still live under one Constitution.

When states honor one another's laws and citizens treat one another as equals, the Union holds. When they don't, freedom frays—not in a thunderclap, but stitch by stitch.

The Founders knew that liberty must be *shared* to survive. Article IV is that pledge in ink: out of many homes, one country—bound by faith, by law, and by the honor of those who keep their word.

📚 Tidbits from Article IV – The States and the Union

🖋 1. Full Faith & Credit
States must recognize other states' public acts, records, and court judgments—marriage licenses, adoptions, contracts, and more.

☞ **Freedom Fact:** Your legal life doesn't reset at a state line.

🏛 2. Privileges & Immunities
A citizen of one state enjoys basic civil rights in every other—no second-class Americans.

☞ **Freedom Fact:** Equality among citizens builds unity among states.

🏛 3. Extradition
Fleeing across a border won't defeat justice; governors cooperate to return accused persons for trial.

☞ **Freedom Fact:** Justice travels faster than flight.

4. New States on Equal Footing

Congress admits new states; each enters with the same sovereignty as the original thirteen.

☞ **Freedom Fact:** Every new star shines with equal brightness.

5. Carving or Combining States

No new state may be formed within another (or by joining states) without consent of the affected legislatures *and* Congress.

☞ **Freedom Fact:** Boundaries change only by agreement, not impulse.

6. Republican Guarantee

The United States guarantees every state a **republican form of government**—no kings, no oligarchs.

☞ **Freedom Fact:** Self-government is not optional; it's guaranteed.

7. Protection from Invasion & Violence

The federal government must help defend states against invasion and, upon request, domestic violence.

☞ **Freedom Fact:** No state stands alone when danger comes.

8. State Courts, National Respect

A final judgment in one state's courts carries weight in another—preventing relitigation games.

☞ **Freedom Fact:** One nation means one standard of justice, honored everywhere.

9. Right to Travel & Work

While not named outright, Article IV undergirds free movement and the right to pursue a livelihood across state lines.

☞ **Freedom Fact:** Opportunity in America is portable.

10. Expansion by Principle, Not Conquest

From the Northwest Ordinance's blueprint to Article IV's protections, growth meant welcoming equals—not ruling provinces.

☞ **Freedom Fact:** We add states as partners, not possessions.

✒ The Ink Well

The Founders wrote with quills, not keyboards — but their ink carried a timeless truth: *unity is a choice.*
Article IV was their reminder that freedom cannot survive in isolation.
Each state's promise to the others made the Republic whole.

Take a quiet moment and write this in your journal or ink well:

───────────── ▄ ─────────────

"What does unity mean to me — and how do I keep faith with my fellow Americans?"

Let your words be your ink, your thoughts the parchment. The Republic lives when its people still choose to write its story together.

🦅 Patriot's Reflection

The Union was never meant to erase the individuality of the states —
only to unite their purpose. Each star on the flag burns with its own
light, yet together they form one constellation — a portrait of freedom
drawn across the heavens.

The Founders built a Republic strong enough to stand together and
wise enough to disagree. Article IV is its quiet guardian, ensuring that
no citizen is foreign in their own land and no state stands alone. It
reminds us that liberty depends not only on independence, but on
interdependence — that strength is born when free people choose
cooperation over division.

When the Constitution was signed, it created not just a government, but
a covenant — that *"We the People"* would remain one people, bound
by faith, by law, and by liberty. Across generations, that inked promise
has weathered storms of war, dissent, and doubt, yet it endures —
shining through the hearts of those who still believe that freedom
requires both courage and unity.

The parchment may have aged, but the promise has not. Its words call
to every American: to remember that unity is not granted — it is
earned, defended, and renewed by those willing to stand for one nation
under God, indivisible, and forever free.

Chapter 8 – Article V: The Power to Amend

"A Living Document, Guarded by Principle."
Article V of the Constitution

 ## Freedom Fact

The Founders knew perfection was impossible. They wrote a Constitution strong enough to last — yet flexible enough to grow.

In their wisdom, they built what history would call the *safety valve of liberty*: a lawful way to correct errors, expand rights, or adapt to change without resorting to revolution. They had witnessed tyranny in monarchs and chaos in mobs — and knew both could destroy a Republic if people had no peaceful path to reform.

Article V was their answer. It was designed not for ease, but for endurance — a process that would test conviction as much as conviction tests the law. Change, they believed, should come not from anger, but from understanding; not from violence, but from virtue.

To amend the Constitution is to speak with the most powerful voice citizens possess — a voice that echoes through every state, every chamber, every generation. The Founders trusted the people to use that voice sparingly, wisely, and always in defense of liberty's core truth: that freedom must grow to survive, yet never grow beyond the bounds of justice.

Through this single article, the Republic gained a living heart — one that beats slower than passion but steadier than time itself.

Through this single article, the Republic gained a living heart — one that beats slower than passion but steadier than time itself, reminding us that change is the servant of liberty, not its master.

A Brief Story

As the Convention of 1787 neared its end, parchment filled with ink and debate hung heavy in the air. The delegates had crafted something bold, but they knew it was not perfect. **Benjamin Franklin**, the elder philosopher among them, rose to speak. His voice was frail, but his wisdom was clear: "I confess that there are several parts of this Constitution which I do not at present approve... but I doubt too whether any other Convention we can obtain may be able to make a better one."

Franklin's humility carried the moment. The men in that room understood — their work would never be beyond error. So they did something extraordinary: they wrote into their masterpiece a mechanism to fix itself.

That mechanism became *the safety valve of the Republic* — Article V. It gave the people and their states a lawful path to vent the pressure of disagreement through debate and amendment rather than through conflict or collapse.

In the years that followed, this clause proved its worth again and again. It produced the Bill of Rights, mended the scars of civil war, expanded suffrage, and extended justice to those long denied it. Every amendment was a release of pressure — not a tear in the fabric, but a stitch strengthening it.

Franklin's closing words still echo through the centuries: "The opinions I have of its errors, I sacrifice to the public good." With that spirit of humility, the Founders left us not a flawless Constitution, but one that could grow wiser with every generation willing to pick up the quill and keep the Republic breathing.

Trivia Time

1 How many methods exist to propose a constitutional amendment?

Answer: Two — either by Congress, **or** by a constitutional convention called by the states. That single word "or" holds great power. It means amendments can begin in Congress *or* through "the several States," a phrase written so future states would share equal authority. If two-thirds of both houses of Congress agree — or two-thirds of the states call for a convention — an amendment may be proposed. It's the people's *safety valve*, shared between state and federal hands.

2 How many votes are required in Congress to propose an amendment?

Answer: A two-thirds vote in both the House and the Senate *or* the several states. This high threshold ensures that change reflects broad national consensus — not passing political winds.

3 How many states must ratify an amendment for it to become law?

Answer: Three-fourths of the states.
Today, that means thirty-eight out of fifty. The Founders designed this to protect liberty from haste — change requires both time and agreement.

4 How many total amendments have been added to the Constitution?

Answer: Twenty-seven.
Of those, the first ten — the Bill of Rights — were ratified together in 1791.

5 Which amendment repealed another?

Answer: The 21st Amendment repealed the 18th, ending Prohibition in 1933.

6 Which amendment gave women the right to vote?

Answer: The 19th Amendment, ratified in 1920.

7 What amendment limits a president to two terms in office?

Answer: The 22nd Amendment, ratified in 1951, following Franklin D. Roosevelt's four elections.

8 Which amendment lowered the voting age to 18?

Answer: The 26th Amendment, ratified in 1971, during the Vietnam War era.

9 Which amendment abolished slavery?

Answer: The 13th Amendment, ratified in 1865 — one of the three "Reconstruction Amendments."

10 Which amendment protects freedom of speech, press, religion, and assembly?

Answer: The 1st Amendment — the cornerstone of the Bill of Rights and the promise of liberty itself.

Amendment Math — The Power of the Several States

Article V gives both Congress *and* the states a voice in changing the Constitution.

- **To Propose an Amendment:** Two-thirds of both houses of Congress (that's 67 Senators and 290 Representatives), **or** two-thirds of the state legislatures — **34 states** — can call for a convention to propose amendments.

- **To Ratify an Amendment:** Three-fourths of the states — **38 out of 50** — must approve before any amendment becomes law.

The phrase **"the several States"** was written so that future states would share the same authority as the original thirteen.
It reminds us that the Constitution belongs not to Washington, D.C., but to *We the People* — acting through our states to keep the Republic free, flexible, and faithful to its founding principles.

A Moment to Reflect

The Founders gave us something no other nation possessed — the right to reshape our own Constitution.
Imagine holding that power today. What principle would you fight to add or defend? Would you stand for a new right, or protect the ones already won? Imagine taking up the same quill the Founders once held. What would you write into the Constitution to strengthen freedom today?

⚔ Challenge Corner

Amending the Constitution takes more than majority rule; it takes national agreement.
Is that difficulty a strength — protecting stability — or a weakness that slows progress?
If you could propose one amendment, what would it be?
Write your idea, and consider how it would hold up under the weight of time and principle.

📖 Did You Know?

Article V was one of the final pieces added to the Constitution — a quiet clause with extraordinary power. It became the **safety valve** of the Republic, giving future generations a peaceful way to repair or refine the nation's charter without resorting to revolution.

The framers understood that no government made by man could ever be perfect. But rather than rewrite the Constitution each time the world changed, they built in a mechanism for thoughtful evolution — one that required both national and state consent. Through amendment, the Constitution could adapt to new challenges while remaining anchored to its founding principles.

Only once has Congress proposed an amendment that nearly reshaped the document itself — the **Equal Rights Amendment**. Though it fell short of ratification, its debate proved that disagreement need not destroy unity. The conversation itself reflected the genius of Article V: that progress in a free nation begins not with force, but with persuasion.

👉 **Freedom Fact:** The Founders made change possible — but only when the people agreed. Article V reminds us that true reform in America moves at the speed of reason, not impulse.

Freedom Reflection – The Courage to Change

The Founders knew that even the best ideas could grow brittle if they could not bend. Article V was their solution — a safety valve built not for rebellion, but renewal.

It gives "We the People" the rarest of powers: to refine our own foundation. Yet, that power was never meant to be easy. Requiring supermajorities across both Congress and the states ensures that only ideas rooted in reason and unity become law.

Every amendment — from the Bill of Rights to the abolition of slavery — carries the same message: freedom is alive. It evolves, corrects, and strengthens itself through honest debate.

Article V reminds us that America is not carved in stone; it is written in ink — living words guided by conscience. Our Republic endures because it can listen, learn, and, when needed, amend itself with both courage and care.

Tidbits from Article V – The Power to Amend

1. Two Paths to Proposal
Amendments can be proposed in two ways — by a two-thirds vote of Congress *or* by a convention called by two-thirds of the states. That word "or" is vital: it keeps power balanced between Washington and the people.

Freedom Fact: The Founders trusted both the government *and* the governed to shape the nation's future.

2. Two Paths to Ratification
An amendment becomes law when three-fourths of the states approve — either through their legislatures or special conventions.

Freedom Fact: No change becomes permanent without overwhelming public agreement.

3. The Difficulty Is the Design
The amendment process was made intentionally hard. Change requires patience, persuasion, and principle — not passion alone.

Freedom Fact: Easy change breeds instability; earned change builds legacy.

4. A Living Document

Since 1789, over 11,000 amendments have been proposed, but only 27 have succeeded. That rarity is proof of the Constitution's strength.

☞ **Freedom Fact:** Endurance, not abundance, defines great laws.

5. State Conventions

Only once — the 21st Amendment ending Prohibition — was ratified by state conventions instead of legislatures, allowing direct input from citizens.

☞ **Freedom Fact:** When the people speak directly, history listens.

6. Permanent Protections

Article V forbids any amendment that would strip a state of its equal representation in the Senate without its consent.

☞ **Freedom Fact:** Equality among states is not negotiable.

7. The First Ten Amendments

The Bill of Rights was the first great test of Article V, proving that liberty could expand without rewriting the Constitution.

☞ **Freedom Fact:** Freedom's foundation was strengthened, not replaced.

8. The Power of Precedent

Each amendment reflects its era — from women's suffrage to term limits — turning national struggle into civic progress.

☞ **Freedom Fact:** Amending the Constitution is history's way of self-correction.

9. The "Several States" Clause

The framers wrote "the convention of the several states" because they didn't yet know how many there would be. Today, it means 34 states must call for a convention to propose amendments.

☞ **Freedom Fact:** The word "several" ensures that the people's voice can always rise from the states, not just the Capitol.

10. The Spirit of Renewal

Every amendment begins with a belief — that the nation can do better. Article V keeps that belief alive, proving that liberty isn't static; it's self-aware.

☞ **Freedom Fact:** The Constitution's heartbeat is the courage to evolve.

The Ink Well

Every amendment began with an idea that someone cared enough to write down.

———————— ▬ ————————

Take your pen — or your quill — and imagine you could add one line to the Constitution.
What would it say about liberty, duty, or unity?

Write it here. Let your words remind you that the story of freedom is still being written.

🦅 Patriot's Reflection

The Constitution's strength lies not in its rigidity, but in its resilience. **Article V** is the Republic's safety valve — the quiet promise that liberty can bend without breaking. It reminds us that a free people do not fear correction; they embrace it. Through this simple yet profound process, the Founders ensured that future generations could repair what time or error might strain, without tearing the document apart.

Each amendment is a reflection of growth — sometimes born of pain, often of courage. From the abolition of slavery to the expansion of voting rights, every inked addition to the parchment tells of a nation humble enough to admit imperfection, yet brave enough to change.

The quills of 1787 may rest, but their spirit endures in every pen raised to defend or amend what they began. For in the *Republic's heartbeat* lies this enduring truth: freedom is not fragile because it can change — it is eternal because it can endure that change.

✒ **Freedom Fact:** A Constitution that cannot change will one day cease to serve; a people who forget how to change it will one day cease to be free.

And so long as a single citizen still believes in liberty, the quill will never run dry.

Chapter 9 — Article VI: The Supremacy of the Constitution

 Freedom Fact

The Founders knew that a nation divided by competing laws could never stand united in liberty.
Under the Articles of Confederation, states ignored treaties, defied Congress, and contradicted one another. The solution was Article VI — the anchor that bound the new Republic to one Constitution, one standard, and one guiding oath.

It established the **Supremacy Clause**, ensuring that federal law, when made constitutionally, would outrank conflicting state laws. Not to silence the states, but to guarantee that every American lived under the same shield of justice.

Article VI is the quiet promise that the rule of law is not a suggestion — it is the foundation of freedom.

A Brief Story

In the years after independence, the states behaved less like a united nation and more like thirteen separate countries.
Some refused to honor treaties. Others issued competing currencies. Court rulings in one state were often ignored in another. One state might jail a debtor while another freed him. A merchant lawful in one port could be a criminal in the next.

The new Republic wobbled under the weight of its own contradictions. Even George Washington warned that the Union was held together only by "a thread."

When the Constitutional Convention gathered in 1787, the delegates carried these failures like scars. They knew that liberty would collapse if every state played by different rules. A country cannot stand firm when its foundation is fractured.

So they crafted Article VI.

It declared that the Constitution — not Congress, not the president, not any state — would be the **supreme law of the land**. Treaties would bind all states. Federal law, when made properly, would hold firm across borders. And officials at every level would swear an oath not to a ruler, but to the Constitution itself — a promise unheard of in a world ruled by kings.

This was revolutionary.
In an age of monarchs and empires, America placed its highest loyalty in **principle**, not power; in **law**, not lineage.

When **George Washington** took the first presidential oath, when the first justices donned their robes, when soldiers raised their hands before heading into battle — each was fulfilling Article VI's quiet command: **Serve the law so the law can serve the people.**

From that anchor grew a nation capable of arguing fiercely yet remaining united — a Republic held together not by force, but by fidelity to a shared foundation.
Article VI turned thirteen quarreling states into one constitutional family, proving that unity is strongest when it is chosen, sworn, and lived.

🕐 Trivia Time

1 What does the Supremacy Clause establish?
Answer: That the Constitution and federal laws made under it are the supreme law of the land.

2 Who must take an oath to support the Constitution?
Answer: All federal and state officials — legislators, judges, and executive officers.

3 Can a religious test be required to hold public office in the United States?
Answer: No — Article VI prohibits religious tests for any office.

4 What problem under the Articles of Confederation made the Supremacy Clause necessary?
Answer: States routinely ignored national laws and treaties.

5 Which landmark case affirmed federal supremacy over state laws?
Answer: McCulloch v. Maryland (1819).

6 What phrase describes the Constitution's role in resolving conflicts between federal and state laws?
Answer: The Constitution is the "final word" or "ultimate authority."

7 What does the Oath Clause require of government officials?
Answer: That they swear loyalty to the Constitution — not to a person, party, or state.

8 Can a state pass a law that contradicts federal law?
Answer: No — if federal law is constitutional, it prevails.

9 What does the prohibition on religious tests protect?
Answer: Freedom of conscience and equal opportunity in public service.

10 Why did the Founders include Article VI?
Answer: To ensure national unity under a single legal foundation, preventing the chaos of competing state laws.

A Moment to Reflect

The Founders asked a bold question:
Can a nation remain free if its loyalty belongs to principles rather than to rulers?

Imagine taking the same oath sworn by presidents, judges, and soldiers — promising to defend not a person, but a document.
What part of the Constitution do you think most needs defending today?
Why does loyalty to principle matter more than loyalty to party?

Write your thoughts, and consider how you would uphold the oath in moments of pressure.

Challenge Corner

Article VI demands unity — but unity grounded in law, not obedience.

If you lived during the early Republic and saw states defying treaties, ignoring courts, and refusing cooperation, would you support a stronger Supremacy Clause?
Or would you fear that federal power might overshadow state independence?

Choose a side and defend it:
Is national unity worth strengthening federal authority, or should states retain more freedom to differ?

Write your stance — and explain how it protects liberty.

Did You Know?

The prohibition on religious tests was one of the most radical ideas of its time.
In 1787, nearly every nation tied political power to a state church. America broke that tradition, declaring that **faith would never be a qualification for freedom.**

The Oath Clause was equally groundbreaking: it ensured that soldiers, lawmakers, and judges would all serve the Constitution, not any leader.

And the Supremacy Clause prevented the young Republic from repeating its greatest failure — the chaos that nearly dissolved the Union under the Articles of Confederation.

Freedom Fact:
Article VI protects unity without erasing diversity — a single Constitution with fifty unique voices beneath it.

Freedom Reflection – The Anchor of the Union

The Supremacy Clause does more than decide which law wins — it keeps the nation whole.
Without Article VI, America would be a patchwork of competing rules, where rights changed at every border and loyalty shifted with every local dispute. The Founders knew that a Republic divided by law could not remain united in liberty.

So they bound every official, from the President to the smallest-town clerk, to a single oath: to preserve, protect, and defend the Constitution.
Not a ruler.
Not a party.
Not a state.
But a principle.

That oath is the invisible backbone of the Republic. It ensures that power bends to law, and that law bends to the Constitution — the people's charter of freedom.

Unity does not mean uniformity. States keep their identities, their cultures, their choices. But Article VI ensures that under all those differences, one foundation remains unshaken.

☞ **Freedom Reflection Thought:**
The Constitution anchors us not because we always agree — but because we always return to the same rulebook.

Tidbits from Article VI

⚖ 1. The Supremacy Clause
Federal law, when constitutional, overrides conflicting state law.

☞ **Freedom Fact:** This keeps all Americans equal under the same protections.

✒ 2. The Oath Clause
All officials must swear loyalty to the Constitution.

☞ **Freedom Fact:** The oath binds leaders to principle, not power.

🕊 3. No Religious Test
No one can be barred from office because of their faith.

☞ **Freedom Fact:** Freedom of conscience is a cornerstone of liberty.

⊕ 4. Binding Treaties
States must honor national treaties made under the Constitution.

☞ **Freedom Fact:** This ensures America speaks with one voice to the world.

🏛 5. State Courts Must Obey Federal Law
Even state judges must follow the Constitution and federal law above their own state laws.

☞ **Freedom Fact:** Local justice cannot contradict national rights.

6. Supremacy Prevents Fragmentation

Without the Supremacy Clause, states could undercut each other's laws and tear the Union apart.

Freedom Fact: The clause protects unity without crushing individuality.

7. Federal Law Still Has Limits

Supremacy applies only when federal law itself is constitutional.

Freedom Fact: Power remains checked by the courts and the people.

8. The Clause Supports Civil Rights

Many civil rights victories relied on federal supremacy over discriminatory state laws.

Freedom Fact: National rights cannot be stripped by local prejudice.

9. The Founders Learned from Failure

The chaos under the Articles of Confederation showed that weak national authority invites conflict and confusion.

Freedom Fact: Article VI fixed the Union's greatest flaw.

10. One Constitution, Many States

The clause binds fifty diverse states into one Republic under a single Constitution.

Freedom Fact: Unity is not uniformity — it's shared commitment.

The Ink Well

The oath of office is not poetry — it is a promise.

———————————— ● ————————————

Imagine you were taking that oath today.
What responsibility would weigh heaviest on your heart?
What part of the Constitution would you feel most bound to defend?

Write one sentence — one line you would vow to uphold — and let it remind you that liberty lives through those who protect it.

🦅 Patriot's Reflection

The strength of America has never come from its rulers, but from its resolve — a shared commitment to live under the same Constitution, no matter our differences.

Article VI is the quiet guardian of that resolve.
It tells us that power must bow to principle, that officials must serve the law, and that no citizen is a stranger in their own country. Every oath sworn, every right upheld, every law tested in court renews the promise made in 1787:
that liberty will never depend on loyalty to a man, but loyalty to an idea.

The Founders knew nations collapse when laws become suggestions and oaths become ornaments.
So they anchored our Republic to something stronger than politics — the supremacy of a Constitution written for all, binding upon all, and entrusted to all.

The parchment has aged, but the promise has not.
Its call remains clear:
Stand firm in principle.
Hold fast to unity.
Remember that freedom endures not through power, but through fidelity to the law that protects us all.

👉 Freedom Fact:
A nation stays free not because its leaders are powerful, but because its people are faithful — to their oath, and to their Constitution.

Chapter 10 – Article VII: The Birth Certificate of the Constitution

"From Proposal to People"
"The Ratification of the Conventions of nine States, shall be sufficient for the Establishment of this Constitution…"
— Article VII, U.S. Constitution

 Freedom Fact

The Founders understood that a Constitution gains power not when it is written, but when it is **accepted**.
Article VII is the nation's *birth certificate* — the rule that transformed a draft on parchment into the supreme law of a living Republic.

Rather than require all thirteen states to agree, the framers chose a bold threshold:
nine states would be enough to launch the new government.

This act of courage prevented a single dissenting state from holding liberty hostage — and ensured that the Union could begin with strength, not stagnation.

👉 **Freedom Fact:** Article VII proves that legitimacy flows from *the consent of the people*, not the comfort of politicians.

A Brief Story

By September of 1787, the delegates at Philadelphia were exhausted.
Four months of arguments, compromises, slammed fists, whispered
deals, and long nights had finally produced a new Constitution.
But paper alone could not save the Republic.

The real battle lay ahead.

When the document left Independence Hall, it entered a nation divided.
Some cheered it as salvation.
Others feared it as tyranny reborn.

Taverns, churches, marketplaces, and homes erupted in debate.
Federalists praised the strong but balanced structure.
Anti-Federalists warned that liberty could vanish under centralized
power.
Newspapers printed fierce essays — some under names like "Publius,"
others under pseudonyms like "Brutus" and "Cato."

But Article VII gave the debate its finish line.
If nine states ratified, the Constitution would become law for all who
joined.
No unanimity required.
No ability for a single holdout to doom the nation.

Delaware raced to approve it first.
Pennsylvania followed, then New Jersey, Georgia, and Connecticut.
By June of 1788, New Hampshire became the crucial ninth — and the
Constitution sprang to life.

Yet two key states — Virginia and New York — had not yet agreed.
Without them, the Republic could still fracture.
James Madison, Alexander Hamilton, John Jay, and countless others
wrote, spoke, and convinced their countrymen that the new
Constitution was the best hope for liberty.

At last, both major states ratified.
The Union held.
A new nation under a new charter was born.

No cannons fired.
No blood spilled.
The Revolution's final victory came not through muskets — but
through *ratification*.

⏰ Trivia Time

1 **How many states were required to ratify the Constitution?**
Answer: Nine.

2 **What year was the Constitution signed?**
Answer: 1787.

3 **Which state ratified the Constitution first?**
Answer: Delaware.

4 **Which state provided the decisive ninth ratification?**
Answer: New Hampshire.

5 **Which two major states hesitated but eventually ratified?**
Answer: Virginia and New York.

6 **What influential essays supported ratification?**
Answer: The Federalist Papers.

7 **Who were the three authors of the Federalist Papers?**
Answer: Alexander Hamilton, James Madison, and John Jay.

8 **Which state was the last to ratify the Constitution?**
Answer: Rhode Island in 1790.

9 **Did Congress or the states ratify the Constitution?**
Answer: State conventions — chosen by the people — not state legislatures.

10 **What document governed America before the Constitution?**
Answer: The Articles of Confederation.

 Did You Know?

Article VII is only one sentence long — yet it launched the most successful governing document in human history.
By requiring ratification through **state conventions**, the framers bypassed politicians and placed the decision directly in the hands of the people.

Freedom Fact:
Article VII proved that the Constitution was not imposed — it was *chosen*.
No king decreed it.
No army enforced it.
It rose because free citizens lifted it.

A Moment to Reflect

Imagine you were a citizen in 1787.
Would you trust a new Constitution after years of revolution, debt, and uncertainty?
Would you fear too much power — or fear too little?

In a world without safety nets, without modern institutions, without guarantees, ratification required courage.
Ask yourself:
What does it take today to preserve something so many risked their future to secure?

Challenge Corner

Put yourself in the shoes of a delegate at a state ratifying convention.
Your neighbors disagree.
Your newspapers battle.
Your vote may shape the destiny of millions yet unborn.

Would you have ratified the Constitution?
What would have convinced you — or concerned you?
Write your reasoning.
History was shaped by ordinary citizens who dared to think deeply.

Tidbits from Article VII

1. Only One Article Required for Ratification

The Founders needed just a single article to establish how the new Constitution would take effect.

Freedom Fact: Ratification was about agreement, not perfection.

2. Nine States Was the Magic Number

The Constitution would become law once **nine of thirteen states** approved it — a bold break from the Articles' requirement of unanimity.

3. Delaware Was First

On December 7, 1787, Delaware earned the nickname **"The First State"** by being the first to ratify.

4. Rhode Island Was Last — and Reluctant

Suspicious of centralized power, Rhode Island refused to attend the Convention and didn't ratify until **May 29, 1790**.

5. Ratification Was Done by Conventions, Not Legislatures

The Founders insisted on state **ratifying conventions** so the people — not politicians — would decide the fate of the Constitution.

Freedom Fact: This was one of the most democratic acts of the entire founding era.

6. Ratification Was Fiercely Debated

Federalists and Anti-Federalists battled in newspapers nationwide. Hamilton, Madison, and Jay wrote the **Federalist Papers** to persuade Americans to adopt the Constitution.

7. New York's Ratification Almost Failed

New York was deeply divided; it ratified by a razor-thin margin. Without its approval, the new nation would have been geographically fractured.

8. The Bill of Rights Was Born From the Debate

Many states ratified only after receiving a promise that amendments protecting individual liberties would follow.

 Freedom Fact: Article VII indirectly gave birth to the Bill of Rights.

 ### 9. Ratification Changed America Overnight

Once nine states approved, the government under the Articles instantly became obsolete — replaced by the Constitution's stronger but balanced framework.

 ### 10. The Final Signature Was Symbolic

Though each state ratified separately, the delegates signed Article VII to declare the Constitution complete. Their signatures marked not a law — but a commitment.

Freedom Reflection – Choosing the Republic

The Constitution did not come to life because a few great men signed it in Philadelphia — it came to life because ordinary citizens, gathered in state conventions, **chose** it.

Article VII is a quiet reminder that power in America does not flow from the top down, but from the bottom up. It took courage for farmers, merchants, veterans, and neighbors to look beyond fear and uncertainty and say, "Yes — we will trust this new framework of liberty."

Ratification was more than a vote on a document. It was a decision about identity:
Would America remain a loose collection of squabbling states, or become a single Republic under one Constitution?

Every generation faces its own version of that choice. We may not sit in ratifying conventions, but we "ratify" the Constitution each time we learn it, defend it, and pass it on. A Republic is never kept by paper alone — it is kept by people who continue to agree that freedom is worth the responsibility.

 ### Freedom Reflection Thought:

The Constitution wasn't just adopted once in 1788 — it is quietly adopted again every time a citizen decides to stand with it.

The Ink Well

———————— 🔹 ————————

Think of a decision in your life that changed everything — not all at once, but slowly, quietly, inevitably.
Article VII was that decision for America.

Write what "ratification" means to you — choosing a path, accepting responsibility, or stepping into the unknown.

🦅 Patriot's Reflection

The Constitution did not become the foundation of our Republic the moment it was drafted — but the moment the people *claimed* it. Article VII is a powerful reminder that self-government is never handed down from the powerful; it rises up from the willing. It affirms that the source of American authority is not Congress, not a president, not even the Founders themselves — but citizens who give their consent freely, knowingly, and deliberately.

In 1788, America did something no empire, monarchy, or dynasty had dared: it placed its future in the hands of ordinary people and waited. No bayonets enforced the Constitution. No king decreed it. The new government would not exist until nine states said, in essence, *"We choose this."* That patient act of humility — government waiting on the governed — became one of the greatest political statements in human history.

And yet, ratification was not inevitable. Debates raged in taverns, churches, newspapers, and crowded meeting halls. Farmers, merchants, veterans, widows, pastors, and tradesmen all wrestled with the same question: *Would this new Constitution protect their liberty better than the Articles that had carried them through war?* In casting their approval, they were not endorsing a document — they were shaping a destiny.

Every generation since has faced its own moment of ratification. Not through formal conventions, but through something just as real: our willingness to uphold the Constitution when it is challenged, misunderstood, or ignored.
Will we defend the principles chosen in that decisive year?
Will we guard the balance of power?
Will we insist that government remains the servant, not the master?

Each of us must decide whether we will be like that ninth state — the one whose choice made liberty real. Article VII is more than a historical footnote; it is a living call to action. It reminds us that a Republic does not survive by tradition or by habit, but by renewal — when the people continue to choose the Constitution as firmly as they did in 1788.

The ink of Article VII still speaks: *A Republic is only as strong as the citizens willing to ratify it again with courage, conviction, and love of country.*

Chapter 11 – The Birth of the Bill of Rights

"A Republic cannot stand unless its people stand for their rights."
— *Founders' Principle, 1791*

 Freedom Fact

The Constitution created the structure of our government —
the Bill of Rights protected the people from that government.

The Founders understood that even the best-designed system could
drift toward tyranny if it wasn't restrained by principles higher than
politics.
So they wrote a list of rights that government could never touch —
speech, faith, privacy, arms, due process, and more.

These protections weren't inventions of government;
they were **rights that pre-existed government itself —**
rooted in natural law, moral duty, and the belief that liberty flows from
God, not kings.

By placing the Bill of Rights at the very front of America's legal
heritage, the Founders ensured that the Constitution would be trusted
not as a tool of power, but as a **guardian of the individual.**

The Bill of Rights became a shield strong enough to resist political
storms and flexible enough to defend every generation yet to come.

It stands as a reminder that:
Freedom is not granted — it is protected.
Liberty is not inherited — it is defended.

A Brief Story

When the Constitution was completed in 1787, not everyone felt secure. Patriot leaders like Patrick Henry and George Mason warned that without a clear list of rights, the new federal government might someday reach further than intended. They wanted guarantees — boundaries that no future Congress or president could cross.

James Madison originally believed the Constitution itself was enough of a safeguard.
But as the states debated ratification, citizens demanded more.
Town meetings, newspaper columns, and state conventions echoed the same message:
"We want our rights in writing."

Listening to the people, Madison gathered more than two hundred suggestions sent by the states and spent long nights organizing them. Ideas overlapped, clashed, and sometimes went too far, but from the mountain of proposals he shaped twelve amendments that balanced liberty with order.

Debates in Congress were passionate.
Should speech be limitless?
Should citizens have the right to bear arms?
Should soldiers ever be quartered in homes?
Should rights not written down still be protected?

On **December 15, 1791**, ten amendments were ratified as the Bill of Rights.
Not privileges — but protections.
Not favors from a government — but limits placed upon it.

The Bill of Rights did more than restrain power.
It reassured a young nation that liberty would never again depend on the goodwill of rulers.
It placed freedom in writing — bold, permanent, and clear — so that every generation would know where their rights begin, and where government ends.

Trivia Time

1 **How many amendments were originally proposed to the states?**
Answer: Twelve.

2 **How many became the Bill of Rights?**
Answer: Ten.

3 **Who is considered the "Father of the Bill of Rights"?**
Answer: James Madison.

4 **What year were the Bill of Rights ratified?**
Answer: 1791.

5 **Which amendment protects freedom of speech and religion?**
Answer: The First Amendment.

6 **Which amendment protects the right to keep and bear arms?**
Answer: The Second Amendment.

7 **Which amendment guards against unreasonable searches and seizures?**
Answer: The Fourth Amendment.

8 **Which amendment guarantees the right to a fair trial?**
Answer: The Sixth Amendment.

9 **Which amendment states that powers not given to the federal government belong to the states or the people?**
Answer: The Tenth Amendment.

10 **Which amendment says the government cannot take your property without fair payment?**
Answer: The Fifth Amendment.

 Did You Know?

Madison first wanted the amendments woven directly into the Constitution.
Congress rejected the idea — they wanted the rights easy to find and impossible to miss.

Several Founders actually feared listing rights,
worried that anything *not listed* might someday be claimed as unprotected.
So the Ninth Amendment declared:
the people possess rights beyond those written down.

 Freedom Fact:
The Bill of Rights does not limit the *people* — it limits the *government*.

 A Moment to Reflect

Imagine being asked to approve the Constitution
without explicit protection for speech, faith, privacy, or firearms.
Would you trust the government enough to leave those freedoms unspoken?

Which rights would *you* refuse to live without?

Write a short note.
What liberty is worth defending most?

⚔ Challenge Corner

Think about a freedom you use daily — your voice, your beliefs, your privacy.
Now imagine if the Bill of Rights had never existed.

Would your life look the same?

Challenge:
Explain the First Amendment to someone younger.
If every American did that once a year, liberty would never be forgotten.

Freedom Reflection – The Soul of Liberty

The Bill of Rights is America's moral compass —
a permanent reminder that the government serves the people,
not the other way around.

The Founders understood a hard truth:
governments grow — and liberty shrinks if citizens sleep.

So they carved ten bright boundaries that no official may cross.
When courts defend them, the Republic stands.
When citizens forget them, freedom fades quietly — not by force,
but by apathy.

👉 Freedom Reflection Thought:
Rights survive only when citizens understand them — and defend them.

Tidbits from the Bill of Rights

1. The First Amendment Holds Five Freedoms
Speech, press, religion, assembly, petition.

2. The Second Amendment Protects Liberty as Well as Life
It was written for defense — of self and of freedom.

3. The Third Amendment Is a Warning from History
British soldiers once lived in colonial homes. Never again.

4. The Fourth Amendment Guards Privacy
Warrants require cause — not convenience.

5. The Fifth Amendment Protects the Accused
Due process, fair compensation, no self-incrimination.

6. The Sixth Amendment Ensures Fair Trials
Speedy, public, impartial — justice in plain sight.

7. The Seventh Amendment Preserves Civil Juries
Civil justice matters too — not just criminal cases.

8. The Eighth Amendment Rejects Cruelty
Punishment must never become oppression.

9. The Ninth Amendment Reserves Unwritten Rights
Your freedoms do not end where the ink stops.

10. The Tenth Amendment Protects Federalism
If power isn't given to Washington, it belongs to the states or the people.

The Ink Well

Which right in the Bill of Rights do you treasure most?
Why does it matter to you?

Write a few thoughts —
your future self will be glad you did.

🦅 Patriot's Reflection

The Bill of Rights is the people's armor — not forged in fire, but in faith… faith that free citizens can govern themselves, and that liberty will outlast any moment of fear.

The Founders knew that rights ignored are rights lost. So they gave future generations a shield — ten amendments strong enough to withstand kings, mobs, and time itself.

They understood that government, even with good intentions, leans naturally toward power.
Only a vigilant people can hold that power in check.

Every amendment in the Bill of Rights is a reminder: freedom is not inherited — it is maintained.
It must be read, defended, debated, and, when necessary, spoken aloud in the face of those who would shrink it.

When you defend these rights, you stand in the same long line of patriots who chose courage over comfort so that America might remain the land of the free.

The ink of those first ten amendments still speaks, and its message is simple: A nation that guards its rights guards its future.

Chapter 12 – The First Amendment: The Five Freedoms

"Congress shall make no law…"
With those four words, the First Amendment erects a wall around liberty — one no king, parliament, or president may cross.

 ## Freedom Fact

The First Amendment protects not one liberty, but **five** —
five pillars strong enough to hold a free society upright.

These freedoms were placed *first* for a reason:
a nation cannot remain free if its people cannot **speak, publish, assemble, worship**, or **petition** without fear.

The Founders believed these rights were not created by government —
they were **protected from** government.
To silence the people would be to silence the Republic itself.

A Brief Story

In the early 1790s, America was a nation still learning to use its voice. The ink on the Constitution was barely dry, yet the air crackled with energy — a young Republic discovering that freedom was not quiet. Newspapers multiplied in every city and crossroads town, each one louder and more partisan than the last. Some praised Washington; others mocked him. Jefferson and Hamilton launched ideas like cannon fire, battling through rival editors who turned political disagreements into daily headlines.

Taverns became the nation's first talk shows. Men argued over mugs of ale; women debated in sewing circles and churchyards. Farmers read broadsheets aloud on courthouse steps. The new Republic was messy, noisy, divided — and wonderfully alive. For the first time in history, ordinary citizens were not whispering opinions behind closed doors; they were shouting them from porches, pulpits, and printing presses.

But with freedom came fear.
As tensions with France rose and partisan battles intensified, Congress passed a series of laws in 1798 that struck at the very heart of American liberty: the Alien and Sedition Acts. Overnight, criticism of the federal government became a crime. Editors were dragged into court. Journalists were jailed. Newspapers were shut down for daring to question those in power. Citizens who had once spoken boldly now weighed every word, wondering whether the wrong sentence could bring a knock at the door.

Then something unmistakably American happened.
People pushed back.

Printers defied the laws and kept publishing. Citizens held meetings, circulated petitions, and refused to let their voices be muffled. Jefferson and Madison drafted the Kentucky and Virginia Resolutions, declaring the acts dangerous and unjust. Farmers, merchants, and veterans who had fought a war for liberty recognized the threat instantly — and they would not surrender the very rights they had bled for.

In the election of 1800, the nation used the only weapon a free people ever truly need: the ballot box. The voters spoke louder than any law could silence. The Sedition Act expired, the jailed editors were released, and the new administration walked into office with a message that echoed far beyond that tumultuous year: In America, power changes hands peacefully — and the people, not the government, decide the limits of speech.

The First Amendment had barely been tested in court, yet it had already proven its purpose. A free people armed with free speech may be challenged, threatened, or pressured — but they will not remain quiet for long.

🧠 Trivia Time

1 **What five freedoms are protected by the First Amendment?**
Answer: Religion, speech, press, assembly, and petition.

2 **What famous phrase describes the separation between government and religion?**
Answer: "A wall of separation between Church and State."

3 **Can the government jail someone for criticizing elected officials?**
Answer: No — political speech is strongly protected.

4 **What is "freedom of the press"?**
Answer: The right to publish ideas and information without government control.

5 **What does the freedom of assembly protect?**
Answer: The right to gather peacefully in groups.

6 **What does "petition the government" mean?**
Answer: Citizens may ask, demand, or urge the government to fix problems.

7 **What early law tested these freedoms in 1798?**
Answer: The Alien and Sedition Acts.

8 **Which Supreme Court case protected students wearing armbands in protest?**
Answer: Tinker v. Des Moines (1969).

9 **Does the First Amendment protect unpopular ideas?**
Answer: Yes — especially those. Popular ideas don't need protection.

10 **Can the government force citizens to say something they disagree with?**
Answer: No — the First Amendment protects against compelled speech.

Did You Know? — First Amendment

The First Amendment protects five freedoms in just forty-five words —
yet those few lines reshaped the destiny of nations.
It was the **first amendment** for a reason: many states refused to ratify
the Constitution unless guarantees of liberty were added.

Early Americans had lived under kings who censored printers, banned
meetings, and punished dissent.
The First Amendment flipped that world upside down — it placed the
citizen above the crown.

Freedom Fact:

These rights are not granted by government; they are **recognitions** of
rights that existed *before* government.
That's why the amendment doesn't say "Congress gives the people…"
— it says **"Congress shall make no law…"** limiting what the people
already possess.

The First Amendment protects the debates of Congress, the voices of
citizens, the sermons of pastors, the pens of journalists, and the
protests of the powerless.
It is the amendment that guards every other amendment — the first line
of defense for a free people.

A Moment to Reflect

Imagine living in a world where:

• criticizing your leaders brings punishment
• your faith is assigned to you
• newspapers print only what they're told
• gatherings require permission
• petitions are treated as threats

Would you call that freedom?

The First Amendment draws the line that separates free nations from all others.
Where would *you* stand if that line were challenged today?

 Challenge Corner

The First Amendment protects speech you agree with —
and speech you don't.

Which is harder?

Think of a viewpoint that frustrates you.
Now imagine defending someone's right to say it anyway.

Write a paragraph reflecting on what real free speech requires:
courage, restraint, and the belief that truth rises best when voices are free.

Freedom Reflection – The Voice of Liberty

The First Amendment is not a luxury — it is the lifeblood of the Republic.

Nations rarely lose freedom in one dramatic moment.
They lose it quietly —
a silenced critic here, a punished newspaper there,
a gathering restricted, a petition ignored.

The Founders wrote the First Amendment to stop that slow erosion.
It protects the voice of the humblest citizen as fiercely as the authority of the greatest.

When these five freedoms thrive, America breathes.
When they weaken, liberty withers.

☞ Freedom Reflection Thought:
A government that can silence the people is a government that no longer serves them.

Tidbits of the First Amendment

1. Five Freedoms in a Single Sentence
Speech, press, religion, assembly, petition.

2. No National Church
The government cannot establish or enforce a state religion.

3. Freedom of Religion Includes Freedom from Religion
No citizen can be compelled to worship or believe.

4. Speech Covers More Than Words
Symbols, clothing, protests, gestures, and art can all be protected speech.

5. The Press Is More Than Newspapers
Blogs, podcasts, digital media, and citizen journalism all fall under its shield.

6. Peaceful Assembly Requires Peace — Not Permission
You may gather publicly without needing government approval.

7. Petition Includes More Than Signatures
Letters, lawsuits, and appeals to any public authority count.

8. Speech Has Limits — But Very Few
Threats, incitement, and defamation are not protected.

9. The First Amendment Restrains Government, Not Citizens
Private platforms or companies are not bound by it.

10. The Founders Placed It First for a Reason
Without voice, every other liberty can be taken silently.

The Ink Well

Write a few lines about a time you spoke up —
or wished you had.

What held you back?
What pushed you forward?

Freedom grows every time a citizen chooses courage over
silence.

🦅 Patriot's Reflection – The Voice That Guards the Republic

The First Amendment is more than ink on parchment —
it is the heartbeat of a free people.

Nations do not lose liberty all at once.
They lose it when citizens begin to whisper instead of speak,
when newspapers fear rather than question,
when gatherings grow quiet and petitions go unread.

The Founders understood that power naturally seeks to silence criticism.
That is why **the very first limit placed on government**
was a command that the people's voice must remain louder than the government's will.

These five freedoms — speech, press, religion, assembly, and petition
— are not weapons of rebellion but instruments of responsibility.
A free nation depends on citizens who speak boldly, think independently,
worship freely, gather openly, and challenge their leaders without fear.

When you exercise these freedoms, you do more than express yourself
— you help preserve the Republic.
You stand in the lineage of patriots who believed that honest voices
are stronger than armies and that truth needs no permission to be spoken.

📜 Patriot's Reflection Thought:
Freedom speaks with your voice —
and the Republic stands only as long as you keep using it.

Chapter 13 – Amendments II & III

The Armed Citizen and the Protected Home

"A well regulated Militia, being necessary to the security of a free State, the right of the people to keep and bear Arms, shall not be infringed."
"No Soldier shall, in time of peace be quartered in any house, without the consent of the Owner…"

 Freedom Fact

The Second and Third Amendments stand side by side for a reason.

The Second protects the **right of the people to keep and bear arms,** ensuring that the citizen is never helpless before force.

The Third protects the **home from becoming an outpost of the military,** forbidding soldiers from being lodged in private houses without consent.

Together, they answer a central fear of the Founders:
that a standing army and a distant government might one day treat citizens as subjects.
These amendments say, in effect:
"The people are not the government's property — and neither are their homes."

🖋 A Brief Story

Before the Revolution, British redcoats marched not only through colonial streets, but into colonial homes.

Under the Quartering Acts, colonists were required to house and feed soldiers, sometimes at their own expense. A man could return from his work to find strangers sleeping in his bed, eating at his table, listening to his private conversations.

At the same time, imperial authorities sought to disarm the people. When British troops marched on Lexington and Concord in 1775, their goal was to seize colonial stores of powder and arms. The shots that followed ignited the War for Independence.

These memories were fresh when the Constitution was written. Patriots who had lived through forced quartering and attempted disarmament would never again allow government troops to occupy their homes or leave them defenseless in their own land.

When James Madison drafted the Bill of Rights, he shaped the Second Amendment to affirm a clear truth:
a free nation requires citizens capable of defending themselves and their liberty.
He shaped the Third to declare that the home is not a barracks —
and the citizen is not a servant of the state.

The tools and uniforms may have changed, but the principle remains the same:
a government that respects its people does not fear an armed citizenry or invade the sanctity of their homes.

⏰ Trivia Time

1 **What event helped spark the American Revolution related to weapons?**
Answer: British attempts to seize colonial arms at Lexington and Concord.

2 **What British law forced colonists to house soldiers?**
Answer: The Quartering Acts.

3 **Who drafted the original text of the Second and Third Amendments?**
Answer: James Madison.

4 **What phrase in the Second Amendment describes the purpose of a militia?**
Answer: "The security of a free State."

5 **What does the Third Amendment forbid in time of peace?**
Answer: Quartering soldiers in private homes without the owner's consent.

6 **When year were the Second and Third Amendments ratified?**
Answer: 1791, along with the rest of the Bill of Rights.

7 **Which amendment is more often discussed in courts today, the Second or the Third?**
Answer: The Second Amendment.

8 **Which Supreme Court case affirmed the individual right to keep and bear arms?**
Answer: District of Columbia v. Heller (2008).

9 **Has the Third Amendment ever been used in a major Supreme Court decision?**
Answer: Rarely — it is one of the least-litigated amendments.

10 **What do these two amendments together protect?**
Answer: The people's ability to defend themselves and the privacy of their homes from military power.

Did You Know? — Second & Third Amendments

The Second and Third Amendments grew directly out of British abuses that helped spark the Revolution.

Before Lexington and Concord, British officers tried to **disarm the colonists** by seizing muskets, powder, and shot. At the same time, the **Quartering Acts** forced families to house and feed soldiers — sometimes in their own bedrooms and kitchens. To the Founders, a government that could disarm you and occupy your home was not a protector — it was a threat.

The Second Amendment answered that threat by affirming that **the people themselves** would never be left powerless.
The Third answered it by declaring that a private home was **not government property**.

Early Americans didn't see these as isolated issues.
To them, arms, home, and liberty were linked: a citizen able to defend his household was a citizen able to defend his freedom.

 ### Freedom Fact:
The word *"infringed"* appears only once in the entire Constitution — in the Second Amendment. The Founders chose it carefully to warn that even small encroachments on this right are dangerous, because freedom is rarely lost all at once — it is usually chipped away.

 ## A Moment to Reflect

Imagine living in a town where soldiers could be ordered into your home and weapons could be taken from your community "for your own good."

Would you feel free?
Would you feel safe?

The Founders believed a truly free people must be able to defend themselves and control who enters their homes — even in times of tension and fear.

⚔ Challenge Corner

Some argue that safety requires more control.
Others argue that safety requires more responsibility and more freedom.

If you had been a delegate in 1791,
would you have voted to protect the right to keep and bear arms
and the right to refuse soldiers in your house?

Write how you would balance safety, responsibility, and liberty
if you had to cast that vote.

🗣 **"The great object is that every man be armed."**
— *Patrick Henry, 1788*

🛡 **"A people armed and free forms the best barrier against the enterprises of ambition."**
— *James Madison*

Freedom Reflection – Power, Boundaries, and the Home

The Second and Third Amendments are not about glorifying weapons or distrusting soldiers —
they are about **drawing boundaries around power**.

The Second says: *the people will never be entirely powerless.*
The Third says: *the home will never be a tool of the state.*

And woven into the Second Amendment are four words that carry the force of a warning and the promise of a protection: **"shall not be infringed."**

"Infringed" appears only once in the entire Constitution —
a deliberate choice.
In the language of the Founding era, it meant **to trespass upon, to encroach, even in the smallest degree**.
The Framers understood that rights are rarely stolen all at once —
they are usually nibbled away, weakened bit by bit, until the people discover too late that they have nothing left to defend themselves with.

That single phrase is a line drawn in firm ink:
government may not chip away at a right the people already possess.

The Founders knew that unchecked force — even wrapped in a uniform — can become a threat to liberty.
So they placed the armed citizen and the protected household
at the heart of the Republic's defenses.

A free nation does not need fearful rulers or helpless citizens.
It needs principled leaders and prepared, responsible people
who understand that **strength and restraint must walk together**.

Freedom Reflection Thought:
A government that respects the people does not fear their strength or invade their homes — and a people who remember their rights cannot be quietly stripped of them.

Tidbits from Amendments II & III

1. The Revolution's Spark
British attempts to seize colonial arms convinced many that disarmament was the first step toward control.

2. "The Militia" Was the People
In the Founders' day, militias were made up of ordinary citizens, not a separate professional army.

3. "Well Regulated" Meant Trained and Ready
The phrase referred to order, discipline, and preparedness — not heavy-handed control.

4. Armed — And Accountable
Many early state laws required able-bodied men to own arms and keep them ready for defense.

5. Home as Sanctuary
The Third Amendment recognizes the home as a protected place against the pressures of military power.

6. A Rarely Litigated Right
The Third Amendment has seen very few court cases, but its presence sends a clear message about boundaries.

7. Fear of Standing Armies
The Founders feared a permanent army that answered only to central power. These amendments push back against that fear.

8. A Principle Older Than America
English history, including the English Bill of Rights of 1689, inspired both the right to arms and resistance to forced quartering.

9. The Tools Changed, The Principle Didn't
From muskets to modern arms, the core idea remains: free citizens must not be left defenseless.

10. Strength Paired with Responsibility
Both amendments assume a people who are strong, disciplined, and moral — capable of wielding power without abusing it.

The Ink Well

What does it mean to you
for a home to be truly "your castle"?
What responsibilities come with the power to defend it?

Write a few lines about how you would explain these two amendments
to someone who has never heard of them.

🦅 Patriot's Reflection

The Second and Third Amendments stand as quiet guardians of a simple truth:
a free people must never be treated as intruders in their own homes or as subjects in their own land.

The Founders had lived under a system where soldiers could be lodged without consent and weapons could be taken without justice.
They vowed that their children and grandchildren would never inherit that kind of fear.

When citizens understand these amendments, they see more than old words about muskets and quarters.
They see a vision of a nation where the doors of a home do not open to power uninvited, and where the people themselves remain the last line of defense for their families, their communities, and their liberty.

👉 Patriot's Reflection Thought:
A nation remains free when its people are strong enough to defend it and wise enough to know why they must.

Chapter 14 – Amendments IV & V: The Shield of the Citizen

"The right of the people to be secure…" — Fourth Amendment

"No person shall… be deprived of life, liberty, or property, without due process of law." — Fifth Amendment

 Freedom Fact

The Fourth and Fifth Amendments form the Constitution's **shield around the individual** — a barrier between the citizen and the power of the state.
They protect privacy, property, and the human voice itself.

The Fourth Amendment guards your **home, papers, and person** against unreasonable searches.
The Fifth protects your **rights, your silence, and your property** from unjust government intrusion.

Together, they declare a profound truth:
In America, the government must knock — and the citizen may say no.

A Brief Story

In the years after independence, memories of British abuses were still sharp.
Soldiers had burst into homes with general warrants — broad permissions allowing them to search anyone, anywhere, without cause. Citizens had been forced to testify against themselves in courts loyal to the Crown. Property had been seized without justice, and silence was treated as guilt.

The Founders refused to repeat those injustices.

So as James Madison shaped the Bill of Rights, he turned the people's anger into protection.
The Fourth Amendment became a wall around privacy: **no search without reason, no seizure without cause, no intrusion without lawful authority.**

The Fifth Amendment went even deeper. It gave every American the right to hold their tongue, the right to due process, and the right to keep their property unless the law — fair, open, and just — said otherwise. It secured the idea that guilt must be proven by the government, not confessed by the accused.

These weren't abstract ideas. They came from lives violated, doors kicked in, and justice denied.
By writing these amendments, the Founders ensured that future generations would never again feel the heavy hand of unchecked authority.

The ink of the Fourth and Fifth Amendments reminds us still: **freedom lives not only in what government may do — but in what it may never do.**

🧠 Trivia Time

1 **What is required for most searches under the Fourth Amendment?**
Answer: A warrant supported by probable cause.

2 **What does the phrase "unreasonable searches and seizures" protect?**
Answer: Your person, home, papers, and personal effects.

3 **What is the legal standard required before a warrant can be issued?**
Answer: Probable cause, sworn under oath.

4 **What protection prevents the government from forcing you to testify against yourself?**
Answer: The Fifth Amendment's right against self-incrimination.

5 **What phrase explains the government's obligation before taking life, liberty, or property?**
Answer: Due process of law.

6 **What is the rule that prevents using illegally obtained evidence at trial?**
Answer: The exclusionary rule.

7 **What must a grand jury decide before someone is charged with a serious federal crime?**
Answer: Whether there is enough evidence for an indictment.

8 **What Fifth Amendment protection relates to being tried twice for the same offense?**
Answer: The protection against double jeopardy.

9 **What power allows government to take private land for public use — with fair compensation?**
Answer: Eminent domain.

10 **Why did the Founders forbid "general warrants"?**
Answer: They allowed unlimited searches — a tool of tyranny the Founders vowed never to repeat.

A Moment to Reflect

Imagine hearing a knock at the door.
Do you feel safe because the government is strong — or because it is limited?

The Founders believed that real security comes not from force, but from freedom.
The Fourth and Fifth Amendments place the burden on government, not the citizen.
They insist that **rights belong to the people first**, and the government must justify every step it takes.

Would you have had the courage, in 1791, to demand these protections — knowing that many believed strong government meant fewer rights?

Challenge Corner

Consider this:
Should privacy ever yield to safety?
Should silence ever be treated as guilt?

Debate the balance with someone you trust.
Where does freedom end and security begin?
The Founders believed those lines must be drawn **carefully** — and always in favor of liberty.

Write your thoughts in the margin or your journal or the ink well— your voice is part of the American conversation the Founders began.

Did You Know?

The Fifth Amendment is one of the most frequently cited provisions in all of American law — not because criminals use it, but because **citizens rely on it** to keep government power in check.

- The phrase **"plead the Fifth"** entered common speech, but its purpose is not to hide guilt — it is to protect the innocent from being forced into a false confession.

- The Founders had watched kings imprison, torture, and coerce people into testifying against themselves. The Fifth Amendment slammed the door on all of it.

- The guarantee of **due process** is why government cannot seize property, imprison a person, or take a life without following clear, lawful procedures.

- And the **takings clause** ("just compensation") ensures that if government ever must take property for public use, citizens are not left powerless or penniless.

Freedom Fact:

The Fifth Amendment is not a loophole — it is a shield. It protects the honest, restrains the powerful, and reminds every branch of government that liberty begins with limits.

Freedom Reflection – Justice With Restraint

Power is never more dangerous than when it believes it is righteous. The Fifth Amendment stands as a warning to every generation: the government may act, but it **must** act justly — even when doing so is inconvenient, slow, or unpopular.

No citizen should fear being forced to speak against themselves.
No person should lose freedom or property without law, process, and proof.
No government should be able to reach into a home or a life without restraint.
The Founders had seen what unchecked authority could do, and they drew a hard boundary around the human soul: *You may accuse, but you must prove. You may govern, but you may not coerce.*

This amendment is the quiet guardian of fairness — the reminder that liberty is not defended only by soldiers or statesmen, but by **rules** that bind power before power binds the people. It protects the innocent, limits the zealous, and ensures that justice rises from evidence, not emotion.

And when the Fifth Amendment is honored, something remarkable happens: the citizen stands tall, and the government stands humble. The courtroom becomes not a stage for the state, but a sanctuary for the individual — a place where truth must earn its authority.

Reflection Thought:

Justice is strongest not when government acts boldly, but when it acts with boundaries. A free nation requires not just good leaders — but good limits.

Tidbits from Amendments IV & V

1. "The right of the people"

The Fourth Amendment begins with the people — not the government.

Freedom Fact: All power starts with the citizen.

2. Probable Cause

Investigations require facts, not suspicion.

Freedom Fact: Hunches don't override liberty.

3. Warrants Must Be Specific

No fishing expeditions — only targeted searches.

Freedom Fact: Specificity prevents abuse.

4. Your Home Is Your Castle

The Founders guarded private homes fiercely.

Freedom Fact: Privacy is a cornerstone of self-government.

5. The Fifth Protects Silence

"No person… shall be compelled to be a witness against himself."

Freedom Fact: Silence is a shield, not an admission.

6. Due Process = Fair Process

The government must follow rules — even when you're accused.

Freedom Fact: Justice must be lawful, not convenient.

7. Grand Juries as Gatekeepers

Before the state can prosecute, citizens must agree.

Freedom Fact: The people restrain the government.

8. Just Compensation

If the government takes property, it must pay fairly.

Freedom Fact: Ownership is protected by law.

9. No Double Jeopardy

One trial per crime — no endless prosecution.

Freedom Fact: Finality is a safeguard of liberty.

10. "Shall Not Be Infringed" of the Legal World

The Fifth Amendment's rules are absolute.

Freedom Fact: Rights protected here cannot be chipped away by convenience.

The Ink Well

The Fourth and Fifth Amendments ask one question that echoes across time:
Where does your freedom begin?

Write your thoughts — what part of yourself do you believe the government must never touch?

🦅 Patriot's Reflection

The Fourth and Fifth Amendments form two pillars of American liberty: **privacy and due process**. They declare that government must prove, justify, and restrain itself before it acts — that power must knock, explain itself, and follow the law like everyone else.

In many nations throughout history, the state has been the master and the citizen merely the subject. But in America, the Constitution reverses that order. Here, the citizen is sovereign, and the government is accountable. These amendments enshrine the idea that freedom begins with personal dignity — with the right to be left alone unless the law, evidence, and due process say otherwise.

They ensure that officials cannot burst through your door, rifle through your belongings, seize your property, or force your confession. They protect the innocent, restrain the zealous, and remind every officer, judge, and legislator that authority must walk the narrow path between necessity and abuse.

Liberty is not always defended on battlefields or in grand speeches. More often, it is preserved quietly — in courtrooms where evidence matters more than accusation, in homes guarded by warrants and privacy, and in the conscience of every citizen who insists that government obey the rules it enforces.

These amendments are not relics; they are guardrails. They preserve the space where ordinary people can live unafraid, speak openly, and stand equal before the law.

The Founders handed you a shield.
Your duty is simple: **carry it well — and never set it down.**

Chapter 15 – Amendments VI, VII & VIII: Justice in the Light

"The accused shall enjoy the right to a speedy and public trial..." — Sixth Amendment

"In suits at common law... the right of trial by jury shall be preserved." — Seventh Amendment

"Excessive bail shall not be required..." — Eighth Amendment

⚖️ Freedom Fact

The Sixth, Seventh, and Eighth Amendments form the **Bill of Rights' courtroom trilogy** — the protections that shield a citizen **after accusation but before judgment**.

They guarantee fairness, transparency, impartial juries, humane treatment, and justice measured by law, not emotion.
They insist that **the government must prove guilt — and must treat the accused as a human being, not an enemy**.

These amendments transformed the courtroom from a chamber of fear into a place where liberty stands watch.

A Brief Story

To understand these amendments, you must step into an 18th-century British courtroom — dark, cramped, and hostile.
The judge served the Crown.
The jurors were handpicked for loyalty.
Trials dragged on for months or happened in secret.
And a simple accusation could ruin a life before the evidence was even heard.

Americans remembered these abuses vividly.

So when Madison crafted the Bill of Rights, he carved out a new vision of justice — one built on light instead of shadows.
The Sixth Amendment guaranteed a **speedy, public trial**, because delays often served the powerful, not the accused.
It required **an impartial jury**, not royal loyalists.
It gave the accused the right to **face their accuser**, to **know the charges**, to **present evidence**, and to **have an attorney** — protections unheard of in much of the world.

The Seventh Amendment preserved the right to a jury in civil cases — a safeguard so important that John Adams called the jury "**the heart and lungs of liberty.**"

Then came the Eighth Amendment, a direct answer to centuries of cruelty:
No excessive bail.
No excessive fines.
No cruel or unusual punishment.
Not in America.

Together, these amendments placed justice in the hands of people — not kings, not officials, not bureaucrats.
They built a courtroom where **truth could breathe and tyranny could not.**

🧠 Trivia Time

1 What amendment guarantees a speedy and public trial?
Answer: The Sixth Amendment.

2 What right does the accused have regarding witnesses?
Answer: To confront them and call their own witnesses.

3 What amendment preserves the right to a jury in civil cases?
Answer: The Seventh Amendment.

4 How many jurors typically serve in a federal criminal trial?
Answer: Twelve.

5 What amendment forbids excessive bail and fines?
Answer: The Eighth Amendment.

6 What type of punishment does the Eighth Amendment prohibit?
Answer: Cruel and unusual punishment.

7 What must the government provide if the accused cannot afford an attorney?
Answer: Court-appointed legal counsel.

8 Why must trials be public?
Answer: To prevent secret abuses of justice.

9 What is the purpose of a jury?
Answer: To ensure verdicts come from citizens, not government officials.

10 What is "due process" in the courtroom context?
Answer: Fair procedures that government must follow before punishment.

⌣ A Moment to Reflect

Imagine standing alone before the full power of the government. Without the Sixth, Seventh, and Eighth Amendments, your voice could be ignored, your trial delayed, your punishment brutal.

These rights are not technicalities — they are protections of your humanity.

If you were accused of a crime, which right would matter most to you?
The jury?
The attorney?
The protection from harsh punishment?

Write your answer — someday, someone may be grateful that you understood.

⚔ Challenge Corner

Debate this with a friend or family member:

Is it better for ten guilty people to go free than for one innocent person to be punished?
Benjamin Franklin said yes. Many disagree.

Where do you stand?
And how do these amendments protect your position?

Your thoughts belong in your journal — they're part of your civic armor.

Did You Know?

The Sixth Amendment doesn't just describe a courtroom —
it **shapes** it.

- The right to a **speedy trial** came from English kings who imprisoned people for years without ever charging them.

- The guarantee of a **public trial** prevents secret justice — the kind used by tyrants to silence opponents.

- The Founders insisted on **an impartial jury**, because a single judge controlled by the crown could never be trusted with a citizen's fate.

- The right to **confront witnesses** keeps accusations honest — no more anonymous whispers sending people to the gallows.

- And the right to **counsel** ensures that the poor and the powerless stand equal with the wealthy in the eyes of the law.

Freedom Fact:
The Sixth Amendment transforms the courtroom from a tool of the state into an arena of fairness — where truth must earn its victory.

"The freedom of the press is the bulwark of liberty; it is only in silence that tyranny begins."

—James Maddison, 1799

Freedom Reflection – Justice in the Light

A nation cannot call itself free if its justice hides in the shadows.
The Sixth Amendment drags the entire process into the light — where juries watch, citizens listen, and truth stands a fighting chance.

It reminds us that accusation is not guilt, that every person deserves a defender, and that government must prove its case openly, honestly, and beyond doubt.

In the Founders' eyes, a courtroom was not a place for the state to flex its power —
but a place where the **individual stands protected** against that power.

Reflection Thought:
When trials are fair, the Republic is strong.
When trials become weapons, freedom begins to fall.

"Reason and free inquiry are the only effectual agents against error." — *Letter to Peter Carr*

—Thomas Jefferson, 1787

Tidbits from Amendments VI, VII & VIII

1. "Speedy" Means Fair, Not Rushed

Trials must move forward without delay.

Freedom Fact: Justice delayed can be justice denied.

2. Public Trials Prevent Abuse

A trial in the open keeps government honest.

Freedom Fact: Sunlight is a disinfectant.

3. The Jury as Citizens' Power

Ordinary Americans decide guilt — not officials.

Freedom Fact: Self-government lives in the jury box.

4. Notice of Charges

You must be told exactly what you're accused of.

Freedom Fact: Vagueness is a tool of tyranny.

5. Confrontation Clause

Accusers must speak openly — no secret testimony.

Freedom Fact: Justice requires clarity.

6. Right to Counsel

The Founders knew that law is too complex to face alone.

Freedom Fact: The accused must never be outmatched.

🧑‍⚖️ 7. Civil Juries Preserve Property Rights

The Seventh Amendment protects disputes between citizens.

Freedom Fact: The courtroom belongs to the people.

💸 8. Excessive Bail Was a Royal Weapon

Kings used high bail to imprison without trial.

Freedom Fact: America broke that chain.

🔥 9. "Cruel and Unusual" Evolves

Punishments once common — whipping, branding — are now considered unconstitutional.

Freedom Fact: Justice grows with moral conscience.

🏛 10. These Amendments Limit Emotion

They prevent punishment driven by anger, fear, or frenzy.

Freedom Fact: Liberty needs cool heads and firm rules.

The Ink Well

———— ▲ ————

Think of a moment when fairness mattered most to you — a disagreement, a punishment, a decision.

Write what "justice" means in your own words.
Your definition is part of America's ongoing story.

🦅 Patriot's Reflection

The Fourth and Fifth Amendments protect your dignity.
The Sixth, Seventh, and Eighth protect your day in court.
Together, they form a shield around every citizen — a reminder that justice is not the privilege of the powerful, but the birthright of the people.

These amendments create a justice system that sees the citizen not as prey, but as equal.
They declare that punishment must be fair, trials must be honest, and truth must not hide behind locked doors. They insist that the state must prove, must justify, and must restrain itself before it lays a hand on the life or liberty of any person.

In America, the government may hold power —
but justice holds the government.
When the courtroom stays open, when juries remain independent, and when rights are honored even in moments of fear, the Republic stands taller than any threat it faces.

For these protections were written not only for the innocent, but for the accused; not only for the respected, but for the forgotten. The Founders knew that a nation is judged not by how it treats the powerful, but by how it treats the vulnerable standing alone before authority.

These amendments remind us that liberty survives only when the courtroom is a place of courage, integrity, and light.
When citizens defend these rights — for themselves and for others — they keep faith with generations who fought to secure them.

Defend these rights, and you defend the Republic itself.

Chapter 16 – Amendments IX & X: The Final Safeguards

"The enumeration... shall not be construed to deny or disparage others retained by the people." — Ninth Amendment

"The powers not delegated... are reserved to the States respectively, or to the people." — Tenth Amendment

⚖️ Freedom Fact

The Ninth and Tenth Amendments are the **guardrails of the Constitution** — the final locks on federal power.

The Ninth protects **rights too numerous to list**, reminding the government that the people possess freedoms beyond the text. The Tenth protects **powers too precious to centralize**, reminding Washington that anything not granted belongs to the states — or directly to the people.

Together, they whisper the same truth:
Liberty is vast. Government is limited. The people remain sovereign.

🪶 A Brief Story

When the Bill of Rights was being written, some delegates worried that listing specific rights might backfire.
"If we write down ten," they argued,
"the government may claim those are the only ten the people possess."

So Madison crafted the Ninth Amendment — a safety clause for liberty.
It declared that the people hold **far more rights than the parchment could contain,** rights woven into nature, conscience, and common sense.

But another challenge waited: power.
Who holds what? Who decides what?
The Constitution gave certain powers to the federal government — coining money, raising armies, making treaties — but what about everything else?

Under the Articles of Confederation, the states nearly tore the nation apart through division and rivalry.
Under the new Constitution, some feared the opposite — that a powerful federal government would swallow the states whole.

The answer became the Tenth Amendment.

It drew a bold line:
If the Constitution doesn't give a power to the federal government, it stays with the states or the people.
Not in Washington.
Not in Congress.
Not in any branch of the federal system.

These two amendments — one guarding rights, the other guarding power — completed the Bill of Rights with precision.
They affirmed that the government's authority begins where the Constitution allows…
and ends where the people say it does.

🧠 Trivia Time

1 What does the Ninth Amendment protect?
Answer: Rights not specifically listed in the Constitution.

2 What does the Tenth Amendment protect?
Answer: Powers not delegated to the federal government.

3 Who retains those unlisted powers?
Answer: The states or the people.

4 Why did some delegates fear a Bill of Rights?
Answer: They feared it would imply the people had only the rights listed.

5 Which amendment was Madison's answer to that fear?
Answer: The Ninth Amendment.

6 What kind of federal power does the Tenth Amendment prohibit?
Answer: Any power not granted by the Constitution.

7 What do the Ninth and Tenth Amendments work together to limit?
Answer: Federal overreach.

8 Who did the Founders intend to be the primary guardians of local matters?
Answer: The states.

9 Which amendment reinforces the principle of popular sovereignty?
Answer: Both — but especially the Tenth.

10 Why are these amendments sometimes called "the People's Amendments"?
Answer: Because they protect what belongs to the people — rights and power.

A Moment to Reflect

Think about this:
The Founders believed that your rights exist **before** government,
and that your power exists **beyond** government.

The Ninth and Tenth Amendments simply remind the government of
what was always true:
the people are the source of authority, not the subjects of it.

Which do you think poses a greater threat today —
a government forgetting your rights,
or a government forgetting its limits?

Your answer matters.

Challenge Corner

Debate this with someone close to you:

**Should the federal government have broad national authority,
or should most decisions remain with the states and the people?**

Where is the balance between unity and liberty?
Between national strength and local control?

Use this space to consider whether our nation has drifted too far from
the Tenth Amendment —
and what it would take to restore that balance.

📘 Did You Know?

The Ninth and Tenth Amendments were written as *guardrails* — not for the people, but for the government.
Many delegates feared that listing specific rights might imply that citizens had **only** those rights.
To prevent this, Madison included the Ninth Amendment, which protects **all rights not written down** — the rights that come from being human, not from being governed.

The Tenth Amendment reinforced the boundary:
if a power isn't given to the federal government, it belongs to the states or to the people.
This ensured that the national government could never grow by assumption — only by permission.

👉 **Freedom Fact (bold as required):**
The Ninth protects your unlisted rights.
The Tenth protects your un-delegated powers.
Together, they form the final shield between liberty and overreach.

Freedom Reflection – The Final Guardrails of Liberty

The Ninth and Tenth Amendments stand as the Constitution's closing defense against the slow creep of government power. They remind us that not all rights can be listed — and not all authority can be claimed. The government has only the powers we grant it.
The people keep everything else.

These amendments form the quiet backbone of American liberty. They protect the rights that belong to every person simply because they exist, and they shield the states from a national government tempted to reach beyond its boundaries. They are the final guardrails that keep freedom from sliding into central control — a reminder that liberty endures only when power remains close to the people who must live under it.

The Ninth Amendment protects the vast territory of human rights that cannot fit on parchment. The Tenth reminds every generation that Washington's reach must not exceed the people's consent. Together, they reaffirm the balance that keeps a Republic strong: a national government capable of defending liberty, and local communities capable of shaping it.

When citizens understand these guardrails, freedom expands. When they forget them, power fills the empty space — slowly, quietly, and often with the best of intentions. That is why these amendments remain so vital today: they teach that the preservation of liberty is not automatic. It requires attention, awareness, and a willingness to insist that government remain within its proper bounds.

Freedom Reflection Thought:
A Republic remains free not because its government is restrained, but because its people insist on doing the restraining.

Tidbits from Amendments IX & X

1. The Ninth Amendment Protects the Unknown

Not all rights can be listed — and they don't have to be.

☞ *Freedom Fact:* You have more rights than the Constitution names.

2. The Tenth Amendment Draws the Line

Power must remain close to the people.

☞ *Freedom Fact:* If Washington wasn't granted the power, it doesn't have it.

3. Federalism Was a Compromise

States kept sovereignty; the nation kept unity.

☞ *Freedom Fact:* Dual power prevents single-point tyranny.

4. "Enumerated Powers" Matters

Congress can act only within listed authorities.

☞ *Freedom Fact:* Limitation protects liberty.

5. The Amendments Work as a Pair

Rights (IX) and powers (X) form a protective circle.

☞ *Freedom Fact:* One guards freedom; the other guards authority.

6. States as Laboratories

States can test ideas without imposing them nationwide.

☞ *Freedom Fact:* Innovation begins locally.

7. The People Are the Final Authority

Both amendments center sovereignty in citizens.

Freedom Fact: Government exists *because* of the people, not over them.

8. This Was a Warning to the Future

The Founders feared creeping centralization.

Freedom Fact: They left us tools to resist it.

9. Madison Called the Ninth "A Rule of Construction"

Meaning: interpret rights generously, not narrowly.

Freedom Fact: The Constitution leans toward liberty.

10. These Amendments Complete the Bill of Rights

They close every loophole for tyranny.

Freedom Fact: Freedom's strongest protections often speak in the quietest words.

✒ The Ink Well

———————— ▲ ————————

What power do you believe the federal government has taken that truly belongs to the states — or to the people?
Write a few thoughts.
Your voice may echo longer than you think.

🦅 Patriot's Reflection

The Ninth and Tenth Amendments remind us that the Constitution was never meant to cage liberty —
it was meant to **chain power**.
They stand at the end of the Bill of Rights like two quiet sentinels, whispering a truth the Founders knew well: freedom grows safest when government grows smallest.

The Founders trusted the people more than politicians,
and trusted local communities more than distant capitals.
They believed that the closer power stayed to the citizen, the safer freedom would remain. These amendments guard that belief, ensuring that rights not written are still protected, and powers not granted are still out of Washington's reach.

These final amendments are more than footnotes —
they are the last guardposts of the Republic,
the final reminder that sovereignty begins with the people and returns to the people. They draw the boundary lines that prevent good intentions from becoming overreach, and strong government from becoming centralized rule.

They ensure that America remains a nation of the people, by the people, and for the people — a nation where the citizen stands above the state, and where every level of authority can still be questioned, limited, and held to account.

The Bill of Rights ends here —
but your duty to defend it never does.
For these final protections are not just historical words; they are living warnings. Each generation must decide whether to guard the limits placed on government or surrender them piece by piece.

Freedom endures when the people remember their power.
And the Republic survives when they insist that government remember its limits.

Epilogue — A Republic Carried Forward

The Bill of Rights ends with a reminder:
Liberty does not survive on parchment — it survives in people.

For sixteen chapters, you have walked through the architecture of American freedom: the articles that shape our government, the amendments that restrain it, the rights that protect the citizen, and the principles that keep power in check. Together, they form the most remarkable political inheritance the world has known — a Constitution rooted not in rulers, but in **sovereignty of the people**.

But the Founders never intended these ideas to be admired from a distance.
They intended them to be *used, defended, argued, practiced*, and *lived*.
A Republic cannot endure merely because it was well designed.
It endures because each generation chooses to keep it.

The final lesson of this book is the same lesson the Founders left for their children: **Freedom survives only when the people remember they are the guardians of it.**

And history has a way of reminding us of that truth in moments almost too perfect to be coincidence.

 ## A Moment in Providence

Fifty years to the day after the Declaration of Independence was adopted — July 4, 1826 — its two greatest architects, **John Adams and Thomas Jefferson**, drew their final breaths.

Adams, on his deathbed in Massachusetts, whispered, *"Thomas Jefferson still survives,"* not knowing his friend had died just hours earlier in Virginia.
Across the young nation, bells tolled and cannons roared in celebration of the country they had built. When the news spread that both men had

passed on that same sacred day, many saw it not as a coincidence, but as providence — a final seal placed upon the birth of the Republic.

 Freedom Reflection:
Their rivalry gave birth to a nation; their reconciliation gave it character. Their final act — departing on the anniversary of liberty itself — reminds every generation that freedom, once born, must be kept alive through unity, courage, and conviction.

The Work of Freedom Continues

The Founders were not perfect. They did not claim to be.
But they built a system that could correct its flaws, refine its principles, and grow with its people. That was their genius — not that they gave us a finished nation, but that they gave us a *framework* capable of creating one.

They understood something essential:
Self-government is not a destination. It is a responsibility.

Every vote, every debate, every peaceful disagreement, every act of citizenship — large or small — keeps the American experiment alive. And every voice that speaks for liberty adds another link to the chain that began in 1776, was shaped in 1787, and continues through you.

✒ Your Place in the Story

This book ends here, but the Republic does not.
You are now part of its ongoing chapter — a chapter written not in ink, but in choices:

Do you cherish your rights?
Do you defend your freedoms?
Do you understand the power you hold as a citizen of a sovereign people?

The Founders lit the torch of liberty.
Every generation must carry it forward.
Now it is your turn.

Thank You

This book was born from miles on the highway, long nights in truck stops, and conversations with strangers who became friends. To each of you — farmers, veterans, truckers, parents, and everyday patriots — thank you for sharing your stories, your worries, your hopes, and your courage.

To the people who prayed for me, encouraged me, and reminded me why freedom matters — thank you.

And to every reader who turns these pages with a desire to understand our nation more deeply: you are the reason I wrote this book.

— Ron Coleman

About the Author

Ron Coleman is a U.S. Air Force veteran, engineer, and long-haul truck driver whose life has woven through the heart of America's working class. Born in California, and raised in Nevada, he learned early the enduring values of hard work, faith, and patriotism.

His professional career began in the early 1980s in telecommunications, where he built and managed long-distance switching centers, microwave systems, and global data networks. Over the next two decades, he rose to serve as Vice President of Operations and Engineering for multiple companies, leading teams across the United States and abroad.

In time, Ron traded the conference room for the open highway. Behind the wheel of his Kenworth, he rediscovered the country he had once served—its vast landscapes, resilient people, and the quiet dignity of everyday Americans. The road became more than a livelihood; it became both classroom and calling.

As the nation faced uncertainty and division, Ron became a witness to the struggles of farmers, business owners, veterans, and families striving to hold on to freedom and hope. His journey through The People's Convoy and his cross-country *Grey Wolf Walk Across America for Freedom* were not simply acts of protest, but missions to carry the voices of those who felt overlooked.

Today, Ron writes and speaks about liberty, faith, and the enduring American spirit. His story is not about politics—it is about conviction, truth, and one man's effort to remind America of the principles that shaped her.

Now retired, Ron lives in Nevada. He still finds peace behind the wheel, taking the occasional local trucking job. Each sunrise over the asphalt reminds him why he rolls: for faith, for freedom, and for the people.

Further Reading

These works provide depth, context, and perspective for readers who wish to continue exploring the ideas that shaped the American Republic:

Essential Primary Sources

Declaration of Independence

Constitution of the United States

Federalist Papers & *Anti-Federalist Papers*

Historical Perspectives

1776 — David McCullough

Miracle at Philadelphia — Catherine Drinker Bowen

Plain, Honest Men — Richard Beeman

On Liberty & Self-Government

Democracy in America — Alexis de Tocqueville

The 5000 Year Leap — W. Cleon Skousen

Liberty and Tyranny — Mark R. Levin

The Federalist Society Primer — (Federalist Society)

The Rights of Man — Thomas Paine

 ## Also by Ron Coleman

An American Patriot's Journey to "**Make America Great Again**"

More than a convoy or a walk across America, this memoir chronicles a broader awakening—one man's effort to call attention to the forces reshaping the nation and the quiet erosion of its foundational principles. Drawing on the People's Convoy and the Grey Wolf Walk for Freedom as tools of the journey, Ron Coleman reflects on faith, liberty, responsibility, and the conversations that unfold when Americans are willing to slow down, listen, and look honestly at the country around them.

Grey Wolf Press
An Independent American Publisher
GreyWolfPress.net